# WHAT IS ESOTERIC CHRISTIANITY?

OCTAVES DRAGONFLY

Octaves Dragonfly
PO Box 679
Cape Vincent, NY 13618
www.octavesdragonfly.com

ISBN: 9798671262902

# γνῶθι σεαυτόν

# Introduction

Esoteric Christianity is an ensemble of Christian theology which proposes that some spiritual doctrines of Christianity can only be understood by those who have undergone certain rites (such as baptism) within the religion. The term esoteric was coined in the 17th century and derives from the Greek ἐσωτερικός (esôterikos, "inner").

These spiritual currents share some common denominators, such as heterodox or heretical Christian theology; the canonical gospels, various apocalyptic literature, and some New Testament apocrypha as sacred texts; and discipline arcane, a supposed oral tradition from the Twelve Apostles containing esoteric teachings of Jesus the Christ.

Greek mysticism influenced many early church theologians such as Clement of Alexandria and Origen.

SOME MODERN SCHOLARS BELIEVE THAT IN THE EARLY STAGES OF PROTO-ORTHODOX CHRISTIANITY, A NUCLEUS OF ORAL TEACHINGS WAS INHERITED FROM PALESTINIAN AND HELLENISTIC JUDAISM. IN THE 4TH CENTURY, IT WAS BELIEVED TO FORM THE BASIS OF A SECRET ORAL TRADITION WHICH CAME TO BE CALLED DISCIPLINE ARCANE. MAINSTREAM THEOLOGIANS, HOWEVER, BELIEVE THAT IT CONTAINED ONLY LITURGICAL DETAILS AND CERTAIN OTHER TRADITIONS WHICH REMAIN A PART OF SOME BRANCHES OF MAINSTREAM CHRISTIANITY. IMPORTANT INFLUENCES ON ESOTERIC CHRISTIANITY ARE THE CHRISTIAN THEOLOGIANS CLEMENT OF ALEXANDRIA AND ORIGEN, THE LEADING FIGURES OF THE CATECHETICAL SCHOOL OF ALEXANDRIA.

REINCARNATION WAS ACCEPTED BY MOST GNOSTIC CHRISTIAN SECTS SUCH AS VALENTINIANISM AND THE BASILIDIANS BUT DENIED BY THE PROTO-ORTHODOX ONE. WHILE HYPOTHETICALLY CONSIDERING A COMPLEX MULTIPLE-WORLD TRANSMIGRATION SCHEME IN DE PRINCIPIIS, ORIGEN DENIES

REINCARNATION IN UNMISTAKABLE TERMS IN HIS WORK AGAINST CELSUS AND ELSEWHERE.

DESPITE THIS APPARENT CONTRADICTION, MOST MODERN ESOTERIC CHRISTIAN MOVEMENTS REFER TO ORIGEN'S WRITINGS (ALONG WITH OTHER CHURCH FATHERS AND BIBLICAL PASSAGES) TO VALIDATE THESE IDEAS AS PART OF THE ESOTERIC CHRISTIAN TRADITION OUTSIDE OF THE GNOSTIC SCHOOLS, WHO WERE LATER CONSIDERED HERETICAL IN THE 3RD CENTURY.

# Hermetic Connection

Hermeticism, also called Hermetics, is a religious, philosophical, and esoteric tradition based primarily upon writings attributed to Hermes Trismegistus ("thrice-greatest Hermes").  These writings have greatly influenced the Western esoteric tradition and were considered to be of great importance during both the Renaissance and the Reformation.  The tradition traces its origin to a prisca theologia, a doctrine that affirms the existence of a single, true theology that is present in all religions and that was given by God to man in antiquity.

Many writers, including Lactantius, Cyprian of Carthage, Marsilio Ficino, Giovanni Pico della Mirandola, Giordano Bruno, Tommaso Campanella, Sir Thomas Browne, and Ralph Waldo Emerson, considered Hermes Trismegistus to

"

BE A WISE PAGAN PROPHET WHO FORESAW THE COMING OF CHRISTIANITY.

MUCH OF THE IMPORTANCE OF HERMETICISM ARISES FROM ITS CONNECTION WITH THE DEVELOPMENT OF SCIENCE DURING THE TIME FROM 1300 TO 1600 AD. THE PROMINENCE THAT IT GAVE TO THE IDEA OF INFLUENCING OR CONTROLLING NATURE LED MANY SCIENTISTS TO LOOK TO MAGIC AND THOSE ARTS (E.G., ALCHEMY, ASTROLOGY) WHICH, IT WAS THOUGHT, COULD PUT NATURE TO THE TEST BY MEANS OF EXPERIMENTS. CONSEQUENTLY, IT WAS THE PRACTICAL ASPECTS OF HERMETIC WRITINGS THAT ATTRACTED THE ATTENTION OF SCIENTISTS. ISAAC NEWTON PLACED GREAT FAITH IN THE CONCEPT OF AN UNADULTERATED, PURE, ANCIENT DOCTRINE, WHICH HE STUDIED VIGOROUSLY TO AID HIS UNDERSTANDING OF THE PHYSICAL WORLD.

THE TERM HERMETIC IS FROM THE MEDIEVAL LATIN HERMETICUS, WHICH IS DERIVED FROM THE NAME OF THE GREEK GOD HERMES.

The synonymous term Hermetical is also attested in the 17th century. Sir Thomas Browne in his Religio Medici of 1643 wrote: "Now besides these particular and divided Spirits, there may be (for ought I know) a universal and common Spirit to the whole world. It was the opinion of Plato and is yet of the Hermeticall Philosophers." (R. M. Part 1:2)

Hermes Trimegistus supposedly invented the process of making a glass tube airtight (a process in alchemy) using a secret seal. Hence, the term "completely sealed" is implied in "hermetically sealed" and the term "hermetic" is also equivalent to "occult" or hidden.

In Late Antiquity, Hermetism emerged in parallel with early Christianity, Gnosticism, Neoplatonism, the Chaldaean Oracles, and late Orphic and Pythagorean literature. These doctrines were "characterized by a resistance to the dominance of either pure rationality or doctrinal faith."

The texts now known as the Corpus Hermeticum are dated by modern translators and most scholars as beginning of 2nd century or earlier. These texts dwell upon the oneness and goodness of God, urge purification of the soul, and expand on the relationship between mind and spirit. Their predominant literary form is the dialogue: Hermes Trismegistus instructs a perplexed disciple upon various teachings of the hidden wisdom.

Renaissance

Plutarch's mention of Hermes Trismegistus dates back to the 1st century AD, and Tertullian, Iamblichus, and Porphyry were all familiar with Hermetic writings.

After centuries of falling out of favor, Hermeticism was reintroduced to the West when, in 1460, a man named Leonardo de Candia Pistoia brought the Corpus

Hermeticum to Pistoia. He was one of many agents sent out by Pistoia's ruler, Cosimo de' Medici, to scour European monasteries for lost ancient writings.

In 1614, Isaac Casaubon, a Swiss philologist, analyzed the Greek Hermetic texts for linguistic style. He concluded that the writings attributed to Hermes Trismegistus were not the work of an ancient Egyptian priest but in fact dated to the 2nd and 3rd centuries AD.

Even in light of Casaubon's linguistic discovery (and typical of many adherents of Hermetic philosophy in Europe during the 16th and 17th centuries), Thomas Browne in his Religio Medici (1643) confidently stated: "The severe schools shall never laugh me out of the philosophy of Hermes, that this visible world is but a portrait of the invisible." (R. M. Part 1:12)

In 1678, however, flaws in Casaubon's dating were discerned by Ralph Cudworth, who argued that

Casaubon's allegation of forgery could only be applied to three of the seventeen treatises contained within the Corpus Hermeticum. Moreover, Cudworth noted Casaubon's failure to acknowledge the codification of these treatises as a late formulation of a pre-existing oral tradition. According to Cudworth, the texts must be viewed as a terminus ad quem and not a terminus a quo. Lost Greek texts, and many of the surviving vulgate books, contained discussions of alchemy clothed in philosophical metaphor.

In the 19th century, Walter Scott placed the date of the Hermetic texts shortly after 200 CE, but W. Flinders Petrie placed their origin between 200 and 500 BC.

In 1945, Hermetic texts were found near the Egyptian town Nag Hammadi. One of these texts had the form of a conversation between Hermes and Asclepius. A second text (titled On the Ogdoad and Ennead)

TOLD OF THE HERMETIC MYSTERY
SCHOOLS. IT WAS WRITTEN IN THE
COPTIC LANGUAGE, THE LATEST AND
FINAL FORM IN WHICH THE EGYPTIAN
LANGUAGE WAS WRITTEN.

ACCORDING TO GEZA VERMES,
HERMETICISM WAS A HELLENISTIC
MYSTICISM CONTEMPORANEOUS WITH THE
FOURTH GOSPEL, AND HERMES
TRESMEGISTOS WAS "THE HELLENIZED
REINCARNATION OF THE EGYPTIAN DEITY
THOTH, THE SOURCE OF WISDOM, WHO
WAS BELIEVED TO DEIFY MAN THROUGH
KNOWLEDGE (GNOSIS)."

GILLES QUISPEL SAYS "IT IS NOW
COMPLETELY CERTAIN THAT THERE
EXISTED BEFORE AND AFTER THE
BEGINNING OF THE CHRISTIAN ERA IN
ALEXANDRIA A SECRET SOCIETY, AKIN TO A
MASONIC LODGE. THE MEMBERS OF THIS
GROUP CALLED THEMSELVES 'BRETHREN,'
WERE INITIATED THROUGH A BAPTISM OF
THE SPIRIT, GREETED EACH OTHER WITH A
SACRED KISS, CELEBRATED A SACRED
MEAL AND READ THE HERMETIC WRITINGS
AS EDIFYING TREATISES FOR THEIR
SPIRITUAL PROGRESS." ON THE OTHER

hand, Christian Bull argues that "there is no reason to identify [Alexandria] as the birthplace of a 'Hermetic lodge' as several scholars have done. There is neither internal nor external evidence for such an Alexandrian 'lodge', a designation that is alien to the ancient world and carries Masonic connotations."

In Hermeticism, the ultimate reality is referred to variously as God, the All, or the One.  God in the Hermetica is unitary and transcendent: he is one and exists apart from the material cosmos. Hermetism is therefore profoundly monotheistic although in a deistic and unitarian understanding of the term.  "For it is a ridiculous thing to confess the World to be one, one Sun, one Moon, one Divinity, and yet to have, I know not how many gods."

Its philosophy teaches that there is a transcendent God, or Absolute, in which humans and the entire universe participate. It also

SUBSCRIBES TO THE IDEA THAT OTHER BEINGS, SUCH AS AEONS, ANGELS AND ELEMENTALS, EXIST WITHIN THE UNIVERSE.

HERMETICISTS BELIEVE IN A PRISCA THEOLOGIA, THE DOCTRINE THAT A SINGLE, TRUE THEOLOGY EXISTS, THAT IT EXISTS IN ALL RELIGIONS, AND THAT IT WAS GIVEN BY GOD TO MAN IN ANTIQUITY. IN ORDER TO DEMONSTRATE THE TRUTH OF THE PRISCA THEOLOGIA DOCTRINE, CHRISTIANS APPROPRIATED THE HERMETIC TEACHINGS FOR THEIR OWN PURPOSES. BY THIS ACCOUNT, HERMES TRISMEGISTUS WAS (ACCORDING TO THE FATHERS OF THE CHRISTIAN CHURCH) EITHER A CONTEMPORARY OF MOSES OR THE THIRD IN A LINE OF MEN NAMED HERMES—ENOCH, NOAH, AND THE EGYPTIAN PRIEST-KING WHO IS KNOWN TO US AS HERMES TRISMEGISTUS.

"AS ABOVE, SO BELOW"

THE ACTUAL TEXT OF THAT MAXIM, AS TRANSLATED BY DENNIS W. HAUCK FROM THE EMERALD TABLET OF HERMES TRISMEGISTUS, IS: "THAT WHICH IS BELOW CORRESPONDS TO THAT WHICH IS ABOVE, AND THAT WHICH IS ABOVE

CORRESPONDS TO THAT WHICH IS BELOW, TO ACCOMPLISH THE MIRACLE OF THE ONE THING." THUS, WHATEVER HAPPENS ON ANY LEVEL OF REALITY (PHYSICAL, EMOTIONAL, OR MENTAL) ALSO HAPPENS ON EVERY OTHER LEVEL.

THIS PRINCIPLE, HOWEVER, IS MORE OFTEN USED IN THE SENSE OF THE MICROCOSM AND THE MACROCOSM. THE MICROCOSM IS ONESELF, AND THE MACROCOSM IS THE UNIVERSE. THE MACROCOSM IS AS THE MICROCOSM AND VICE VERSA; WITHIN EACH LIES THE OTHER, AND THROUGH UNDERSTANDING ONE (USUALLY THE MICROCOSM) A PERSON MAY UNDERSTAND THE OTHER.

ALCHEMY (THE OPERATION OF THE SUN): ALCHEMY IS NOT MERELY THE CHANGING OF LEAD INTO GOLD. IT IS AN INVESTIGATION INTO THE SPIRITUAL CONSTITUTION, OR LIFE, OF MATTER AND MATERIAL EXISTENCE THROUGH AN APPLICATION OF THE MYSTERIES OF BIRTH, DEATH, AND RESURRECTION. THE VARIOUS STAGES OF CHEMICAL DISTILLATION AND FERMENTATION, AMONG OTHER PROCESSES, ARE ASPECTS OF

THESE MYSTERIES THAT, WHEN APPLIED, QUICKEN NATURE'S PROCESSES IN ORDER TO BRING A NATURAL BODY TO PERFECTION. THIS PERFECTION IS THE ACCOMPLISHMENT OF THE MAGNUM OPUS (LATIN FOR "GREAT WORK").

ASTROLOGY (THE OPERATION OF THE STARS): HERMES CLAIMS THAT ZOROASTER DISCOVERED THIS PART OF THE WISDOM OF THE WHOLE UNIVERSE, ASTROLOGY, AND TAUGHT IT TO MAN. IN HERMETIC THOUGHT, IT IS LIKELY THAT THE MOVEMENTS OF THE PLANETS HAVE MEANING BEYOND THE LAWS OF PHYSICS AND ACTUALLY HOLD METAPHORICAL VALUE AS SYMBOLS IN THE MIND OF THE ALL, OR GOD. ASTROLOGY HAS INFLUENCES UPON THE EARTH, BUT DOES NOT DICTATE OUR ACTIONS, AND WISDOM IS GAINED WHEN WE KNOW WHAT THESE INFLUENCES ARE AND HOW TO DEAL WITH THEM.

THEURGY (THE OPERATION OF THE GODS): THERE ARE TWO DIFFERENT TYPES OF MAGIC, ACCORDING TO GIOVANNI PICO DELLA MIRANDOLA'S APOLOGY, COMPLETELY OPPOSITE OF EACH OTHER.

THE FIRST IS GOËTIA (GREEK: γοητεια), BLACK MAGIC RELIANT UPON AN ALLIANCE WITH EVIL SPIRITS (I.E., DEMONS). THE SECOND IS THEURGY, DIVINE MAGIC RELIANT UPON AN ALLIANCE WITH DIVINE SPIRITS (I.E., ANGELS, ARCHANGELS, GODS).

"THEURGY" TRANSLATES TO "THE SCIENCE OR ART OF DIVINE WORKS" AND IS THE PRACTICAL ASPECT OF THE HERMETIC ART OF ALCHEMY. FURTHERMORE, ALCHEMY IS SEEN AS THE "KEY" TO THEURGY, THE ULTIMATE GOAL OF WHICH IS TO BECOME UNITED WITH HIGHER COUNTERPARTS, LEADING TO THE ATTAINMENT OF DIVINE CONSCIOUSNESS.

REINCARNATION IS MENTIONED IN HERMETIC TEXTS. HERMES TRISMEGISTUS ASKED:

O SON, HOW MANY BODIES HAVE WE TO PASS THROUGH, HOW MANY BANDS OF DEMONS, THROUGH HOW MANY SERIES OF REPETITIONS AND CYCLES OF THE STARS, BEFORE WE HASTEN TO THE ONE ALONE?

HERMES EXPLAINS IN BOOK 9 OF THE CORPUS HERMETICUM THAT NOUS (REASON AND KNOWLEDGE) BRINGS

FORTH EITHER GOOD OR EVIL, DEPENDING UPON WHETHER ONE RECEIVES ONE'S PERCEPTIONS FROM GOD OR FROM DEMONS. GOD BRINGS FORTH GOOD, BUT DEMONS BRING FORTH EVIL. AMONG THE EVILS BROUGHT FORTH BY DEMONS ARE: "ADULTERY, MURDER, VIOLENCE TO ONE'S FATHER, SACRILEGE, UNGODLINESS, STRANGLING, SUICIDE FROM A CLIFF AND ALL SUCH OTHER DEMONIC ACTIONS".

THIS PROVIDES EVIDENCE THAT HERMETICISM INCLUDES A SENSE OF MORALITY. HOWEVER, THE WORD "GOOD" IS USED VERY STRICTLY. IT IS RESTRICTED TO REFERENCES TO GOD.  IT IS ONLY GOD (IN THE SENSE OF THE NOUS, NOT IN THE SENSE OF THE ALL) WHO IS COMPLETELY FREE OF EVIL. MEN ARE PREVENTED FROM BEING GOOD BECAUSE MAN, HAVING A BODY, IS CONSUMED BY HIS PHYSICAL NATURE, AND IS IGNORANT OF THE SUPREME GOOD.

A FOCUS UPON THE MATERIAL LIFE IS SAID TO BE THE ONLY THING THAT OFFENDS GOD:

AS PROCESSIONS PASSING IN THE ROAD CANNOT ACHIEVE ANYTHING THEMSELVES

YET STILL OBSTRUCT OTHERS, SO THESE MEN MERELY PROCESS THROUGH THE UNIVERSE, LED BY THE PLEASURES OF THE BODY.

ONE MUST CREATE, ONE MUST DO SOMETHING POSITIVE IN ONE'S LIFE, BECAUSE GOD IS A GENERATIVE POWER. NOT CREATING ANYTHING LEAVES A PERSON "STERILE" (I.E., UNABLE TO ACCOMPLISH ANYTHING).

COSMOGONY

A CREATION STORY IS TOLD BY GOD TO HERMES IN THE FIRST BOOK OF THE CORPUS HERMETICUM. IT BEGINS WHEN GOD, BY AN ACT OF WILL, CREATES THE PRIMARY MATTER THAT IS TO CONSTITUTE THE COSMOS. FROM PRIMARY MATTER GOD SEPARATES THE FOUR ELEMENTS (EARTH, AIR, FIRE, AND WATER). THEN GOD ORDERS THE ELEMENTS INTO THE SEVEN HEAVENS (OFTEN HELD TO BE THE SPHERES OF MERCURY, VENUS, MARS, JUPITER, SATURN, THE SUN, AND THE MOON, WHICH TRAVEL IN CIRCLES AND GOVERN DESTINY).

"THE WORD (LOGOS)" THEN LEAPS FORTH FROM THE MATERIALIZING FOUR

ELEMENTS, WHICH WERE UNINTELLIGENT. NOUS THEN MAKES THE SEVEN HEAVENS SPIN, AND FROM THEM SPRING FORTH CREATURES WITHOUT SPEECH.  EARTH IS THEN SEPARATED FROM WATER, AND ANIMALS (OTHER THAN MAN) ARE BROUGHT FORTH.

THE GOD THEN CREATED ANDROGYNOUS MAN, IN GOD'S OWN IMAGE, AND HANDED OVER HIS CREATION.

MAN, CAREFULLY OBSERVED THE CREATION OF NOUS AND RECEIVED FROM GOD MAN'S AUTHORITY OVER ALL CREATION.  MAN, THEN ROSE UP ABOVE THE SPHERES' PATHS IN ORDER TO BETTER VIEW CREATION.  HE THEN SHOWED THE FORM OF THE ALL TO NATURE.  NATURE FELL IN LOVE WITH THE ALL, AND MAN, SEEING HIS REFLECTION IN WATER, FELL IN LOVE WITH NATURE AND WISHED TO DWELL IN IT.  IMMEDIATELY, MAN BECAME ONE WITH NATURE AND BECAME A SLAVE TO ITS LIMITATIONS, SUCH AS SEX AND SLEEP.  IN THIS WAY, MAN BECAME SPEECHLESS (HAVING LOST "THE WORD") AND HE BECAME "DOUBLE", BEING MORTAL IN BODY YET IMMORTAL IN SPIRIT,

AND HAVING AUTHORITY OVER ALL CREATION YET SUBJECT TO DESTINY.

AN ALTERNATIVE ACCOUNT OF THE FALL OF MAN, PRESERVED IN THE DISCOURSES OF ISIS TO HORUS, IS AS FOLLOWS:

GOD, HAVING CREATED THE UNIVERSE, THEN CREATED THE DIVISIONS, THE WORLDS, AND VARIOUS GODS AND GODDESSES, WHOM HE APPOINTED TO CERTAIN PARTS OF THE UNIVERSE. HE THEN TOOK A MYSTERIOUS TRANSPARENT SUBSTANCE, OUT OF WHICH HE CREATED HUMAN SOULS. HE APPOINTED THE SOULS TO THE ASTRAL REGION, WHICH IS JUST ABOVE THE PHYSICAL REGION.

HE THEN ASSIGNED THE SOULS TO CREATE LIFE ON EARTH. HE HANDED OVER SOME OF HIS CREATIVE SUBSTANCE TO THE SOULS AND COMMANDED THEM TO CONTRIBUTE TO HIS CREATION. THE SOULS THEN USED THE SUBSTANCE TO CREATE THE VARIOUS ANIMALS AND FORMS OF PHYSICAL LIFE. SOON AFTER, HOWEVER, THE SOULS BEGAN TO OVERSTEP THEIR BOUNDARIES; THEY SUCCUMBED TO PRIDE AND DESIRED TO BE EQUAL TO THE HIGHEST GODS.

God was displeased and called upon Hermes to create physical bodies that would imprison the souls as a punishment for them. Hermes created human bodies on Earth, and God then told the souls of their punishment.  God decreed that suffering would await them in the physical world, but He promised them that, if their actions on Earth were worthy of their divine origin, their condition would improve, and they would eventually return to the heavenly world.  If it did not improve, He would condemn them to repeated reincarnation upon Earth.

Tobias Churton, Professor of Western Esotericism at the University of Exeter, states, "The Hermetic tradition was both moderate and flexible, offering a tolerant philosophical religion, a religion of the (omnipresent) mind, a purified perception of God, the cosmos, and the self, and much positive encouragement for the spiritual seeker, all of which the

STUDENT COULD TAKE ANYWHERE."
Lutheran Bishop James Heiser
recently evaluated the writings of
Marsilio Ficino and Giovanni Pico
della Mirandola as an attempted
"Hermetic Reformation".

Hermeticists generally attribute
42 books to Hermes Trismegistus,
although many more have been
attributed to him. Most of them,
however, are said to have been lost
when the Great Library of
Alexandria was destroyed.

There are three major texts that
contain Hermetic doctrines:

The Corpus Hermeticum is the most
widely known Hermetic text.  It has
18 chapters, which contain
dialogues between Hermes
Trismegistus and a series of other
men.  The first chapter contains a
dialogue between Poimandres (who
is identified as God) and Hermes.  This
is the first time that Hermes is in
contact with God.  Poimandres
teaches the secrets of the universe
to Hermes.  In later chapters,

HERMES TEACHES OTHERS, SUCH AS HIS SON TAT AND ASCLEPIUS.

THE EMERALD TABLET OF HERMES TRISMEGISTUS IS A SHORT WORK WHICH CONTAINS A PHRASE THAT IS WELL KNOWN IN OCCULT CIRCLES: "AS ABOVE, SO BELOW." THE ACTUAL TEXT OF THAT MAXIM, AS TRANSLATED BY DENNIS W. HAUCK, IS: "THAT WHICH IS BELOW CORRESPONDS TO THAT WHICH IS ABOVE, AND THAT WHICH IS ABOVE CORRESPONDS TO THAT WHICH IS BELOW, TO ACCOMPLISH THE MIRACLE OF THE ONE THING". THE EMERALD TABLET ALSO REFERS TO THE THREE PARTS OF THE WISDOM OF THE WHOLE UNIVERSE. HERMES STATES THAT HIS KNOWLEDGE OF THESE THREE PARTS IS THE REASON WHY HE RECEIVED THE NAME TRISMEGISTUS ("THRICE GREAT" OR "AO-AO-AO" [WHICH MEAN "GREATEST"]). AS THE STORY IS TOLD, THE EMERALD TABLET WAS FOUND BY ALEXANDER THE GREAT AT HEBRON, SUPPOSEDLY IN THE TOMB OF HERMES.

THE PERFECT SERMON (ALSO KNOWN AS THE ASCLEPIUS, THE PERFECT DISCOURSE, OR THE PERFECT TEACHING)

WAS WRITTEN IN THE 2ND OR 3RD CENTURY AD AND IS A HERMETIC WORK SIMILAR IN CONTENT TO THE CORPUS HERMETICUM.

OTHER IMPORTANT ORIGINAL HERMETIC TEXTS INCLUDE THE DISCOURSES OF ISIS TO HORUS, WHICH CONSISTS OF A LONG DIALOGUE BETWEEN ISIS AND HORUS ON THE FALL OF MAN AND OTHER MATTERS; THE DEFINITIONS OF HERMES TO ASCLEPIUS; AND MANY FRAGMENTS, WHICH ARE CHIEFLY PRESERVED IN THE ANTHOLOGY OF STOBAEUS.

THERE ARE ADDITIONAL WORKS THAT, WHILE NOT AS HISTORICALLY SIGNIFICANT AS THE WORKS LISTED ABOVE, HAVE AN IMPORTANT PLACE IN NEO-HERMETICISM:

THE KYBALION: HERMETIC PHILOSOPHY IS A BOOK ANONYMOUSLY PUBLISHED IN 1912 BY THREE PEOPLE WHO CALLED THEMSELVES THE "THREE INITIATES" AND CLAIMS TO EXPOUND UPON ESSENTIAL HERMETIC PRINCIPLES.

A SUGGESTIVE INQUIRY INTO HERMETIC PHILOSOPHY AND ALCHEMY WAS WRITTEN BY MARY ANNE ATWOOD AND ORIGINALLY PUBLISHED ANONYMOUSLY IN 1850. THIS

BOOK WAS WITHDRAWN FROM CIRCULATION BY ATWOOD BUT WAS LATER REPRINTED, AFTER HER DEATH, BY HER LONGTIME FRIEND ISABELLE DE STEIGER. ISABELLE DE STEIGER WAS A MEMBER OF THE GOLDEN DAWN.

A SUGGESTIVE INQUIRY WAS USED FOR THE STUDY OF HERMETICISM AND RESULTED IN SEVERAL WORKS BEING PUBLISHED BY MEMBERS OF THE GOLDEN DAWN:

ARTHUR EDWARD WAITE, A MEMBER AND LATER THE HEAD OF THE GOLDEN DAWN, WROTE THE HERMETIC MUSEUM AND THE HERMETIC MUSEUM RESTORED AND ENLARGED. HE EDITED THE HERMETIC AND ALCHEMICAL WRITINGS OF PARACELSUS, WHICH WAS PUBLISHED AS A TWO-VOLUME SET. HE CONSIDERED HIMSELF TO BE A HERMETICIST AND WAS INSTRUMENTAL IN ADDING THE WORD "HERMETIC" TO THE OFFICIAL TITLE OF THE GOLDEN DAWN.

WILLIAM WYNN WESTCOTT, A FOUNDING MEMBER OF THE GOLDEN DAWN, EDITED A SERIES OF BOOKS ON HERMETICISM TITLED COLLECTANEA

HERMETICA. THE SERIES WAS PUBLISHED BY THE THEOSOPHICAL PUBLISHING SOCIETY.

INITIATION INTO HERMETICS IS THE TITLE OF THE ENGLISH TRANSLATION OF THE FIRST VOLUME OF FRANZ BARDON'S THREE-VOLUME WORK DEALING WITH SELF-REALIZATION WITHIN THE HERMETIC TRADITION.

WHEN HERMETICISM WAS NO LONGER ENDORSED BY THE CHRISTIAN CHURCH, IT WAS DRIVEN UNDERGROUND, AND SEVERAL HERMETIC SOCIETIES WERE FORMED. THE WESTERN ESOTERIC TRADITION IS NOW STEEPED IN HERMETICISM. THE WORK OF SUCH WRITERS AS GIOVANNI PICO DELLA MIRANDOLA, WHO ATTEMPTED TO RECONCILE JEWISH KABBALAH AND CHRISTIAN MYSTICISM, BROUGHT HERMETICISM INTO A CONTEXT MORE EASILY UNDERSTOOD BY EUROPEANS DURING THE TIME OF THE RENAISSANCE.

A FEW PRIMARILY HERMETIC OCCULT ORDERS WERE FOUNDED IN THE LATE MIDDLE AGES AND EARLY RENAISSANCE.

Hermetic magic underwent a 19th-century revival in Western Europe, where it was practiced by groups such as the Hermetic Order of the Golden Dawn, Aurum Solis, and Ragon.  It was also practiced by individual persons, such as Eliphas Lévi, William Butler Yeats, Arthur Machen, Frederick Hockley, and Kenneth M. Mackenzie.

Many Hermetic, or Hermetically influenced, groups exist today. Most of them are derived from Rosicrucianism, Freemasonry, or the Golden Dawn.

Rosicrucianism is a movement which incorporates the Hermetic philosophy.  It dates back to the 17th century. The sources dating the existence of the Rosicrucians to the 17th century are three German pamphlets: the Fama, the Confessio Fraternitatis, and The Chymical Wedding of Christian Rosenkreutz. Some scholars believe these to be hoaxes and say that later Rosicrucian organizations are the

FIRST ACTUAL APPEARANCE OF A ROSICRUCIAN SOCIETY.  THIS ARGUMENT IS HARD TO SUSTAIN GIVEN THAT ORIGINAL COPIES ARE IN EXISTENCE, INCLUDING A FAMA FRATERNITATIS AT THE UNIVERSITY OF ILLINOIS AND ANOTHER IN THE NEW YORK PUBLIC LIBRARY.

THE ROSICRUCIAN ORDER CONSISTS OF A SECRET INNER BODY AND A PUBLIC OUTER BODY THAT IS UNDER THE DIRECTION OF THE INNER BODY.  IT HAS A GRADED SYSTEM IN WHICH MEMBERS MOVE UP IN RANK AND GAIN ACCESS TO MORE KNOWLEDGE.  THERE IS NO FEE FOR ADVANCEMENT.  ONCE A MEMBER HAS BEEN DEEMED ABLE TO UNDERSTAND THE TEACHING, HE MOVES ON TO THE NEXT HIGHER GRADE.

THE FAMA FRATERNITATIS STATES THAT THE BROTHERS OF THE FRATERNITY ARE TO PROFESS NO OTHER THING THAN "TO CURE THE SICK, AND THAT GRATIS".

THE ROSICRUCIAN SPIRITUAL PATH INCORPORATES PHILOSOPHY, KABBALAH, AND DIVINE MAGIC.

THE ORDER IS SYMBOLIZED BY THE ROSE (THE SOUL) AND THE CROSS (THE

BODY). THE UNFOLDING ROSE REPRESENTS THE HUMAN SOUL ACQUIRING GREATER CONSCIOUSNESS WHILE LIVING IN A BODY ON THE MATERIAL PLANE.

UNLIKE THE SOCIETAS ROSICRUCIANA IN ANGLIA, THE HERMETIC ORDER OF THE GOLDEN DAWN WAS OPEN TO BOTH SEXES AND TREATED THEM AS EQUALS. THE ORDER WAS A SPECIFICALLY HERMETIC SOCIETY THAT TAUGHT ALCHEMY, KABBALAH, AND THE MAGIC OF HERMES, ALONG WITH THE PRINCIPLES OF OCCULT SCIENCE.

THE GOLDEN DAWN MAINTAINED THE TIGHTEST OF SECRECY, WHICH WAS ENFORCED BY SEVERE PENALTIES FOR THOSE WHO DISCLOSED ITS SECRETS. OVERALL, THE GENERAL PUBLIC WAS LEFT OBLIVIOUS OF THE ACTIONS, AND EVEN OF THE EXISTENCE, OF THE ORDER, SO FEW IF ANY SECRETS WERE DISCLOSED.

ITS SECRECY WAS BROKEN FIRST BY ALEISTER CROWLEY IN 1905 AND LATER BY ISRAEL REGARDIE IN 1937. REGARDIE GAVE A DETAILED ACCOUNT OF THE

ORDER'S TEACHINGS TO THE GENERAL PUBLIC.

REGARDIE HAD ONCE CLAIMED THAT THERE WERE MANY OCCULT ORDERS WHICH HAD LEARNED WHATEVER THEY KNEW OF MAGIC FROM WHAT HAD BEEN LEAKED FROM THE GOLDEN DAWN BY THOSE WHOM REGARDIE DEEMED "RENEGADE MEMBERS".

THE STELLA MATUTINA WAS A SUCCESSOR SOCIETY OF THE GOLDEN DAWN.

HERMETICISM REMAINS INFLUENTIAL WITHIN ESOTERIC CHRISTIANITY, ESPECIALLY IN MARTINISM.  INFLUENTIAL 20TH CENTURY AND EARLY 21ST CENTURY WRITERS IN THE FIELD INCLUDE VALENTIN TOMBERG AND SERGEI O. PROKOFIEFF.  THE KYBALION SOMEWHAT EXPLICITLY OWED ITSELF TO CHRISTIANITY, AND THE MEDITATIONS ON THE TAROT WAS ONE IMPORTANT BOOK ILLUSTRATING THE THEORY AND PRACTICE OF CHRISTIAN HERMETICISM.

HERMETICISM REMAINS INFLUENTIAL WITHIN NEOPAGANISM, ESPECIALLY IN HELLENISM.  ALSO, IT CAN BE SEEN AS A SORT OF PROTOTYPE OR FIRST VERSION

OF THE LATER 18TH CENTURY FREEMASONRY.  BOTH SHARING THE CENTRAL ELEMENTS OF GNOSTIC AND OCCULT INITIATION AND THE CULT OF TRANSGENDERISM OR DOUBLE GENDERISM SYMBOLIZED BY THE SO CALLED "UNIVERSAL ANDROGYNE" AND/OR THE GOAT HEADED BAPHOMET.

# The Mystery Initiate

In 200 A.D. Saint Clement of Alexandria wrote his book The Stromata; in it, he writes

"The mysteries of the faith are not to be divulged to all. It is requisite... to hide in a mystery the wisdom spoken, which the son of God taught."

— St. Clement of Alexandria, The Stromata, ch. 12 (circa 200 AD)

Saint Clement is pointing towards the topic of our course: Esoteric Christianity.

The word esoteric has the root eso, which means interior or within. Esoteric, coming from the Greek word esotericos, means:

- Intended to be revealed only to the initiates of a group.
- Understood by or meant for only the select few who have special knowledge or interest.
- Belonging to the select few.

Saint Clement is telling us that there are mysteries within the Christian Doctrine, and they are not normally exposed, unless you have had some type of special teaching.

We can find within the New Testament what Jesus states about the mysteries.

In Matthew 13 it is written:

10 And the disciples came and said to Him, "Why do You speak to them in parables?"

11 He answered and said to them, "Because it has been given to you to know the mysteries of the kingdom of heaven, but to them it has not been given."

Normally, everyone seems to think that these mysteries are exposed by some simple reading of the Bible. Actually, the word itself, mystery, μυστήριον (MUSTÉRION) IN GREEK, MEANS "SOMETHING SECRET."

MYSTERY MEANS:

1. SOMETHING OF WHICH INITIATION IS NECESSARY
2. A MYSTERY OR SECRET DOCTRINE;
3. FROM MUSTÉS (ONE INITIATED)

SAINT CLEMENT IS TELLING US THAT THERE ARE THOSE THAT ARE INITIATED, AND THEY CAN UNDERSTAND THE MYSTERIES. JESUS IS SAYING THAT THERE ARE SOME WHO ARE INITIATED INTO HIS TEACHINGS AND THEY UNDERSTAND THE MYSTERY, BUT FOR THOSE WHO ARE NOT INITIATED, WHAT THEY UNDERSTAND IS SOMETHING ELSE, THEY UNDERSTAND IT AT THEIR OWN LEVEL.

THIS IS THE POWER OF THE PARABLE. IN FACT, THE FULL QUOTE OF SAINT CLEMENT IS AS FOLLOWS:

"THE MYSTERIES OF THE FAITH ARE NOT TO BE DIVULGED TO ALL. BUT SINCE THIS TRADITION IS NOT PUBLISHED ALONE FOR HIM WHO PERCEIVES THE MAGNIFICENCE OF THE WORD; IT IS REQUISITE, THEREFORE, TO HIDE IN A MYSTERY THE

WISDOM SPOKEN, WHICH THE SON OF GOD TAUGHT."

— ST. CLEMENT OF ALEXANDRIA, THE STROMATA, CH. 12 (CIRCA 200 AD)

IN OTHER WORDS, THERE ARE DIFFERENT TYPES OF PEOPLE, SOME WHO ARE READY, SOME WHO PERCEIVE THE TRUE MAGNIFICENCE OF THE WORLD. THIS IS ST. CLEMENT ALLUDING TO THE INITIATES, THOSE WHO ARE INITIATED INTO THAT MYSTERY, INTO UNDERSTANDING ESOTERIC CHRISTIANITY. FOR THOSE WHO ARE NOT READY, THEY UNDERSTAND A LESSER TEACHING, A TEACHING THAT IS MORE APPROPRIATE FOR THEM.

IF WE GO TO THE OLD TESTAMENT, WHICH IS, OF COURSE, IS THE TORAH, WE FIND MORE EVIDENCE. THE FIRST FIVE BOOKS OF THE OLD TESTAMENT ARE THE TORAH OF JUDAISM. THE MYSTICAL COMMENTARY OF THE ZOHAR WRITES

ALL MATTERS IN THE TORAH ARE OF A SUPERIOR NATURE AND ARE UPPERMOST SECRETS.

WOE TO THOSE WICKED WHO SAY THAT THE TORAH IS MERELY A STORY AND

NOTHING MORE, FOR THEY LOOK AT THE DRESS AND NO FURTHER.

— ZOHAR, BAMIDBAR 152A

SO, THE MYSTERIOUS, INITIATED, OR ESOTERIC DOCTRINE OF CHRISTIANITY FINDS ITS ROOTS IN THE OLD TESTAMENT, WHICH ALSO HAS AN ESOTERIC DOCTRINE.

SAINT PAUL IN THE 1:3 CORINTHIANS SAYS

AND I, BRETHREN, COULD NOT SPEAK TO YOU AS TO SPIRITUAL PEOPLE BUT AS TO CARNAL, AS TO BABES IN CHRIST.

I FED YOU WITH MILK AND NOT WITH MEAT; FOR UNTIL NOW YOU WERE NOT ABLE TO RECEIVE IT, AND EVEN NOW YOU ARE STILL NOT ABLE...

— 1 CORINTHIANS 3:1-2

DURING THIS TIME IT WAS VERY IMPORTANT TO KEEP THOSE WHO WERE NOT PREPARED FOR THE ESOTERIC DOCTRINE, TO GIVE THEM A TEACHING WHICH WOULD HELP PREPARE THEM; AND FOR THOSE WHO WERE PREPARED, IT WAS IMPORTANT TO GIVE THEM THAT SAME INNER ESOTERIC DOCTRINE WE HAVE BEEN SPEAKING ABOUT.

The very beautiful nature of the Bible, and many of the scriptures, is that both of those teachings are within the same books, within the same scriptures. And, as Jesus states, those who have ears to hear it, and eyes to see it, they see the level of teaching they can comprehend. As Paul states, some are not ready for the meat, they are not ready for the solid food, they are ready for the milk.

So, this is the way it has been for a long time. Unfortunately, the modern forms of Christianity that are popular and prevalent deny an esoteric aspect to Christianity. Just as the Zohar has stated, what happens is that they inherit only the cloak, only the outer dress of the teachings, which are good, but only for a certain level. They have lost the inner doctrine, the esoteric form of Christianity.

Without the esoteric level of the teachings, the tradition as a whole suffers incoherence. If you literally

READ THE BIBLE, YOU WILL FIND ALL SORTS OF CONTRADICTIONS. FOR SOMEONE WHO CRITICALLY ANALYZES THAT — IF THERE IS NO INNER TEACHING — ALL THAT CAN BE SEEN IS SOMETHING THAT CONTRADICTS ITSELF OR SOMETHING THAT APPEARS SUPERFICIAL. THIS IS THE MAIN REASON WHY MANY PEOPLE HAVE LEFT THEIR TRADITIONAL RELIGION, BECAUSE THEY CAN ONLY FIND THE LOWER LEVEL, THE MILK, AND THEY ARE READY TO RECEIVE THE SOLID FOOD, THE MEAT.

THERE ARE GOOD, LEGITIMATE REASONS TO HAVE AN INNER DOCTRINE, BUT TODAY THINGS HAVE OBVIOUSLY CHANGED QUITE A BIT FROM 2,000 YEARS AGO. TODAY WE SEE WE LIVE IN AN AGE OF INFORMATION, FOR TODAY IT IS MORE IMPORTANT TO SET THAT INFORMATION CORRECT, BECAUSE NOT EVERYBODY THAT CLAIMS TO POSSESS THE INNER TEACHINGS LEGITIMATELY HAS THEM. SO, WE NEED TO CLARIFY EXACTLY WHAT THIS ESOTERIC CHRISTIANITY IS, AND THAT'S THE PURPOSE OF THIS COURSE.

We must come to recognize an esoteric Christianity has existed and that such an esoteric Christianity must exist, because as we said, different types of people exist, and we need to have a different type of doctrine available for all of those types of people. There are many people today who view the Bible as taught, as something very simplistic, incoherent, and not substantial. Those people end up leaving the religion because they don't find a level of guidance appropriate for them. This is how many people end up looking for something deeper, and indeed there is an esoteric Christianity.

For us, it is not a debate, it is not a question; it is a living reality. With that being said, let us make some differentiation between the exoteric (outer) traditional forms of Christianity as it is normally known and esoteric Christianity.

In traditional forms of Christianity, there is the doctrine of

JUSTIFICATION, WHICH DEFINES THE REMOVING OF OUR GUILT AND PENALTY OF SIN AND MAKING THE SINNER RIGHTEOUS AGAIN. THE CORE IDEA IS THAT THE LIFE OF JESUS CHRIST ATONED FOR ALL THE SINS OF THE WORLD, AND THROUGH EITHER FAITH ALONE (IF YOU ARE A PROTESTANT), OR GOOD WORKS BASED UPON FAITH, THIS JUSTIFICATION IS ACCOMPLISHED. IN THIS INTERPRETATION, THERE IS A SUBSTITUTIONARY ATONEMENT THAT THE LIFE AND WORKS, THE DRAMA OF JESUS CHRIST, MADE. THE ATONEMENT, BECAUSE JESUS DIED ON THE CROSS, THE SINS OF ALL OF US ARE WASHED AWAY. THIS IS VIEWED, IN THE EXOTERIC WAY, AS A HISTORICAL FACT.

FROM INNER, ESOTERIC CHRISTIANITY, ALL OF THIS MUST BE UNDERSTOOD AS SOMETHING HAPPENING WITHIN OUR HEART AND MIND, WITHIN OUR SOUL AND SPIRIT. YES, JESUS CHRIST INDEED WAS (AND CONTINUES TO BE) A PERSON OF GREAT EXULTATION WHO PROVIDES THE TEACHING AND THE WAY. BUT THE EVENTS OF THE NEW TESTAMENT ARE NOT MERELY A HISTORICAL RECOUNTING. THOSE

EVENTS OF THE NEW TESTAMENT ARE POINTING TOWARDS SPIRITUAL REALITIES THAT MUST OCCUR WITHIN OURSELVES.

ALL OF THE CHARACTERS OF THE BIBLE ARE RELATED TO CERTAIN ASPECTS OF OURSELVES. IN ESOTERIC CHRISTIANITY WHAT IS MEANT BY THE "WORLD" IS OUR OWN INNER WORLD. SO, JESUS, THIS MASTER OF HISTORY, THIS HISTORICAL MASTER, IS TEACHING ABOUT THE INNER JESUS CHRIST, WHICH IS AN ELEMENT OR PRINCIPLE WITHIN OURSELVES.

THAT PRINCIPLE MUST COME INTO OUR WORLD, IN ORDER TO WASH AWAY ALL OF OUR MISTAKES, AND WE PLAY AN ACTIVE PART OF THAT. THIS IS SOMETHING WE MUST PERFORM, SOMETHING WE MUST DO, AND IT IS A PATH OF INTENSE STRUGGLE AND PROFOUND WORKS WITHIN OURSELVES, AND, THROUGH THOSE WORKS, WE ARE ABLE TO KNOW AND COMPREHEND THE NATURE OF DIVINITY.

IN TRADITIONAL, EXOTERIC FORMS OF CHRISTIANITY, INQUIRING WITHIN ONESELF TO DISCOVER AND FUNDAMENTALLY CHANGE ONE'S INNER CONDITION, TO ELIMINATE ALL OF THE SINS OF OUR MIND

AND HEART, IS SEEN AS SOMETHING IMPOSSIBLE FOR THE INDIVIDUAL TO DO. INSTEAD, ONE MUST SIMPLY DO GOOD WORKS OR HAVE A BELIEF, AND WHATEVER NEEDS TO HAPPEN WITHIN ONE'S SELF WILL HAPPEN BY GOD'S WILL.

THE ESOTERIC ASPECT AND TEACHINGS STATES THAT WE ACTUALLY HAVE TO MAKE AN ACTIVE EFFORT TO LOOK WITH OURSELVES, TO TRANSFORM OURSELVES, AND WE DO THAT ONLY THROUGH THE COOPERATION OF THE LORD. WE CAN DO IT, BECAUSE WE HAVE A SPARK OF INNER DIVINITY WITHIN US. THAT SPARK IS THE SOURCE OF OUR GRACE. IT IS THE GIFT OF GOD THAT ALLOWS US TO WORK WITHIN OURSELVES, THAT WE ARE CAPABLE OF MAKING THESE TRANSFORMATIONS WITHIN OURSELVES.

THE LORD IS COOPERATING WITH OUR SPIRITUAL WORK. THERE IS AN ASPECT, A SPARK OF DIVINITY WITHIN US, WHICH CONNECTS US TO THE UNIVERSAL COSMIC FORCE CALLED CHRIST. AND THEREFORE, WE MUST DO THIS WORK, WE MUST FIND THAT CONNECTION WITHIN OURSELVES.

This is what esoteric Christianity is always pointing towards.

From a traditional exoteric perspective, it is seen that the individual is not capable of radically transforming their self. The mind is viewed as a den of thieves, that one should not dwell within one's mind too much, that it is the "devil's playground."

From an esoteric standpoint, we agree that the mind is a den of thieves, and it is the devil's playground, but it is precisely for that reason we must begin to pay attention to all that is happening within our self. Through the cooperation of Christ, through the capability of that divine spark which we have, we are able to develop, and grow, and multiply the light within our self.

We are capable of eliminating (with the cooperation of the Lord) all that is which is not the truth, all of the lying and sinning qualities of our mind. And what comes forth is light,

AND CONSCIOUSNESS, AND UNIVERSAL COMPASSION, AND ALL OF THE BEAUTIFUL QUALITIES THAT WE STRIVE FOR.

EXOTERIC CHRISTIANITY TEACHES A LOT OF VERY GOOD THINGS, A LOT OF NECESSARY THINGS ABOUT HOW TO LIVE A GOOD LIFE, HOW TO PRODUCE A STABLE LIFE, HOW TO LIVE IN THIS WORLD. BUT IT DOES NOT TEACH, AND DOES NOT PERMIT, IN MOST CASES, THE INNER WORKING, THE DEVELOPMENT OF ONE'S OWN SOUL WITHIN. IT DOES NOT VIEW THE SOUL AS SOMETHING THAT MUST BE DEVELOPED, AND THIS IS ONE OF THE PRIMARY DIFFERENCES BETWEEN EXOTERIC CHRISTIANITY AND ESOTERIC CHRISTIANITY.

ESOTERIC CHRISTIANITY VIEWS THE SOUL AS SOMETHING THAT MUST BE WORKED WITH, THAT WE MUST DEVELOP OUR SOUL, AND THAT OUR WORKS AND EFFORTS ARE VERY NECESSARY. IT IS NOT THAT ONE CAN, THROUGH THEIR EGOTISTICAL WILL, FIND SALVATION, NO. BUT IT IS NECESSARY FOR US TO DO GOOD WORKS AND TRANSFORM OUR STATE OF MIND THROUGH A CONTEMPLATIVE

LIFESTYLE, TO TRANSFORM OUR SELF THROUGH THE POWER AND GLORY OF GOD. THE EFFORTS THAT TAKE PLACE WITHIN ESOTERIC CHRISTIANITY ARE IMPOSSIBLE WITHOUT GOD.

UNLIKE THE TRADITIONAL FORMS OF CHRISTIANITY, WE MUST LEARN IN ESOTERIC CHRISTIANITY TO WORK UPON ONE'S SELF, TO INQUIRE WITHIN OUR MIND, TO ELIMINATE OUR DEFECTS. OUR SIDE OF THE WORK IS JUST AS IMPORTANT AS GOD'S SIDE OF THE WORK. IN ESOTERIC CHRISTIANITY, IT IS UNDERSTOOD THAT WE CAN KNOW AND EXPERIENCE GOD DIRECTLY. THIS IS ONE OF THE MAIN DIFFERENCES.

IN THE TRADITIONAL FORMS OF CHRISTIANITY, GOD CAN ONLY BE UNDERSTOOD OR EXPERIENCED THROUGH THE CONDUIT OF THE CHURCH. IN TERMS OF EXOTERIC CHRISTIANITY, GOD CAN ONLY BE UNDERSTOOD WITHIN THE CONFINES OF THE CHURCH, THAT THE CHURCH AND THE CONSECRATED PRIESTS, AND BISHOPS AND CARDINALS ARE THE CONDUIT FROM GOD TO MAN.

Every church believes that they are the "special" church, and they are the physical exponent of the Lord's greatness. Different churches believe they are the one and only holy church of this or that. A Protestant viewpoint is that you need the true, right, correct belief in Jesus, and that is the conduit or the pathway to salvation.

Esoteric Christianity states that we must come to know God. Not only can we know God directly, not only can we comprehend the nature of God, but moreover we must do that. That is the whole point of esoteric Christianity, to fully develop the soul. The full development of the soul is possible, Christ enters into the soul that has been completely purified and developed.

From the traditional, exoteric forms of Christianity, Christ is seen as a person of history, someone who came and who is still in heaven, still active, and believing in that is what is most important.

In esoteric Christianity, what is important is to incarnate Christ. In esoteric Christianity, Christ is not a person; Christ is an energy. Christ, truly, is beyond energy. Christ is a universal comic principle. Christ is the source of universal compassion.

Jesus, whom we call Christ, is a particular spiritual Master, Jesus was a real true Rabbi. He purified his soul to such a degree that the Christ incarnated within him. He taught that, and when he spoke, literally he was speaking the words of Christ.

Χριστός (Christ): Christos, "the Anointed One," and Krestos, whose esoteric meaning is "fire." The word Christ is a title, not a personal name.

What is Christ? Christ comes from a Greek word christos, and christos means one who is anointed, meaning anointed with an oil. Christ from an esoteric standpoint means fire. Christ from an esoteric standpoint is a title. It is not a personal name;

Christ is not a person. So, Jesus was and is a person who acquired or incarnated this universal fire, this universal force, this universal light which is Christ.

In Luke 12 it is written:

"I [Christ] am come to send fire on the earth..." — Luke 12:49

This is the mission of Christ. In esoteric Christianity, all of the events of the Bible need to be understood as something within.

In traditional Christianity, all those events took place literally outside in the world. Actually, all of those events were all parables. There really is no exact, literal historical truth in the Bible.

There are certain events that occurred in the past, and those who were initiated into these teachings would take the literal events and mingle them with esoteric truths, with profound truths, and they would display and write down a history that would give a meaning for those who are not initiated. It is

A VERY GOOD MEANING THAT WAS OFTEN RELATED TO PHYSICAL TRUTHS, BUT NEVER THE LITERAL TRUTH.

THE BIBLE HAS NEVER BEEN A NEWSPAPER, AND IT SHOULD NOT BE READ LIKE A NEWSPAPER. IT SHOULD BE READ IN TERMS OF PARABLES, IN TERMS OF SPIRITUAL TEACHINGS AND TRUTHS. IF YOU UNDERSTAND IT AT A LOWER LEVEL, IT TEACHES YOU HOW TO LIVE WITHIN THE WORLD IN A VERY GOOD WAY. IF YOU UNDERSTAND IT IN THE ESOTERIC LEVEL, IT TEACHES YOU HOW TO TRANSFORM YOUR SOUL, AND HOW TO ACQUIRE ALL THE POWERS, ALL THE COGNIZANCE, ALL THE WISDOM, ALL OF THE COMPASSION, ALL OF THE BEAUTY AND GLORY OF THE SOUL. THIS IS WHAT WE ARE CALLED TO DO, THIS IS THE ESOTERIC PATH OF CHRISTIANITY.

WE FIND IN LUKE CHAPTER 11:

"WOE UNTO YOU, YOU KNOWERS OF THE LAW [TORAH]! FOR YE HAVE TAKEN AWAY THE KEY OF KNOWLEDGE [γνῶσις, GNOSIS]: YE ENTERED NOT IN YOURSELVES, AND THEM THAT WERE ENTERING IN YE HINDERED."

— LUKE 11:52

The knowers of the law have taken away the key of knowledge. Knowledge in the original language is gnosis. Gnosis is written in Greek, which is γνῶσις (gamma nu omega sigma iota sigma) which in English letters you can translate as g-n-o-s-i-s. Gnosis.

Gnosis is knowledge. What tends to happen, and what Jesus was talking about, was that these esoteric teachings have become lost for various reasons. Jesus states that those who knew these teachings were not giving them properly, they were holding onto them too jealously, and they themselves were not living those inner teachings, and they were not teaching others. So, he said, "ye entered not in yourselves, and not in them that were entering, ye hindered".

Gnosis is a word that has been used by a lot of different groups, and it is where we get the word Gnostic. There has been a lot said

ABOUT GNOSTICS, IT IS VERY DIFFICULT TO UNDERSTAND, BASED ON WHAT HAS BEEN WRITTEN ABOUT GNOSTICS, TO REALLY UNDERSTAND WHAT GNOSTICISM ACTUALLY IS. UNFORTUNATELY, THERE IS A LOT OF GROUPS, ANCIENT AND MODERN, WHO STATE THEY ARE GNOSTIC BUT REALLY, THEY ARE NOT. THEY REALLY DON'T HAVE THESE TEACHINGS; THEY HAVE DEGENERATED THEM. AND THERE ARE OTHERS WHO WROTE ABOUT THE GNOSTICS, AGAIN, ANCIENT AND CONTEMPORARY, WHO NEVER UNDERSTOOD THE SECRET KNOWLEDGE, THEY WERE NEVER INITIATED INTO THE SECRET TEACHINGS. THEREFORE, THEY COULD NOT TELL THE DIFFERENCE BETWEEN THOSE GNOSTICS WHO WERE REALLY DEGENERATED, AND THOSE GNOSTICS WHO WERE ACTUALLY HOLDING UP THE MANTLE OF THE TRUE ESOTERIC TEACHING.

OF ALL THE WRITINGS ABOUT GNOSTICS, IT IS VERY DIFFICULT TO GET SOME CLEAR UNDERSTANDING, AND A LOT OF PEOPLE HAVE A NEGATIVE CONNOTATION CONCERNING THE

GNOSTICS. BUT HERE WE CAN SEE THAT A GNOSTIC IS SOMEONE WHO HAS GNOSIS, AND GNOSIS IS SPIRITUAL KNOWLEDGE. SUCH IS THE TRUE MEANING IN ACCORDANCE WITH ESOTERIC CHRISTIANITY.

JESUS WAS BORN IN A SECT CALLED THE ESSENES, WHICH WAS AN ESOTERIC SECT OF JUDAISM. FROM THERE, HE WAS INITIATED INTO THE MYSTERIES, AND OF COURSE MANY OTHER THINGS HAPPENED DURING ALL OF THOSE YEARS WHICH ARE NOT ACCOUNTED FOR IN THE BIBLE. WHEN JESUS CAME TO TEACH, HE CAME TO TEACH A VERY PROFOUND TEACHING, AND MANY PEOPLE WERE NOT AGREEABLE TO THAT, EACH IS WHY THERE IS ALL OF THE DRAMA THAT IS GOING ON.

WE MUST UNDERSTAND THE NEW TESTAMENT AS AN ACCOUNTING OF EVENTS THAT ARE OCCURRING WITHIN OUR HEART AND MIND. WHEN THESE TEACHINGS COME INTO US, WE TRY TO CHANGE AS A PERSON. WE TRY TO BECOME PERFECT AS OUR FATHER IN HEAVEN IS PERFECT, BUT IT IS VERY DIFFICULT. THERE ARE ASPECTS OF

YOURSELF WHICH DON'T WANT TO CHANGE. THERE ARE ASPECTS OF US, WHICH IS LIKE A TYRANT, THAT DOESN'T WANT TO HEAR THESE THINGS, THAT DOESN'T WANT TO CHANGE, IT JUST WANTS TO DO WHATEVER IT WANTS TO DO. THIS IS OUR EGO.

THE EGO IS OUR PERSONAL SATAN. SO, NOT ONLY IS ALL OF THE CHARACTERS, ALL OF THE PROPHETS ALL THE TEACHERS OF THE BIBLE RELATED TO SPIRITUAL ELEMENTS WITHIN US, BUT ALL OF THE NEGATIVE THINGS IN THE BIBLE ARE ALSO RELATED TO NEGATIVE ASPECTS WITHIN OURSELVES.

SATAN IS WITHIN OUR SELF AND WE HAVE TO WORK TO ELIMINATE SATAN. IN 1:2 CORTHINIANS PAUL WRITES:

6 HOWBEIT WE SPEAK WISDOM [σοφία, SOPHIA] AMONG THEM THAT ARE PERFECT [τελείοις, TELEIOS]: YET NOT THE WISDOM OF THIS WORLD, NOR OF THE PRINCES OF THIS WORLD, THAT COME TO NAUGHT:

7 BUT WE SPEAK THE WISDOM OF GOD IN A MYSTERY [μυστήριον, MUSTÉRION], EVEN THE HIDDEN [ἀποκρύπτω, APOKRUPTÓ] WISDOM [σοφία, SOPHIA],

WHICH GOD ORDAINED BEFORE THE WORLD UNTO OUR GLORY…

— 1 Corinthians 2

Obviously, Paul was initiated into these teachings, Paul knew the esoteric doctrine. There are many people who only want to associate the word Gnostic with a particular time frame, but really the best way to understand what a Gnostic is, is someone who has the esoteric teachings. This is because the word gnostic comes from Gnosis, and Gnosis means hidden knowledge. So, Paul, legitimately, was Gnostic.

The original church founded by Jesus had the esoteric teachings, so it was a Gnostic Catholic Church, a truly universal church. That is what the word 'catholic' actually means: something that is universal. The universal knowledge, that is within us, that can set us free.

As it is stated, the truth shall set us free, but we have to come to know that truth within ourselves. The secret teachings are pointing

TOWARDS A SECRET TRUTH WITHIN OUR SELF. WE HAVE TO DISCOVER THE TRUTH WITHIN OUR SELF, BUT THAT TRUTH IS OBSCURED, IT IS HIDDEN, IT IS DIFFICULT TO ACCESS.

IN ORDER TO ACCESS THAT TRUTH, YOU HAVE TO BEGIN TO LIVE LIFE IN A CERTAIN WAY. YOU HAVE TO DO CERTAIN TYPES OF PRACTICES, BECAUSE ANY TYPE OF REAL GNOSTIC, ANYBODY WHO IS TRULY LIVING ESOTERICALLY, THE ESOTERIC CHRISTIAN DOCTRINE, THIS PERSON IS A CONTEMPLATIVE, THIS PERSON IS SOMEONE WHO IS MEDITATING, GOING 'WITHIN'.

MANY PEOPLE BELIEVE THAT MEDITATION IS ONLY SOMETHING THAT BELONGS TO THE EAST, OF COURSE, THIS IS WRONG. ANYONE WHO HAS STUDIED THE PHILOKALIA OR THE CHRISTIAN DESERT FATHERS WOULD KNOW THAT THERE IS TREMENDOUS WISDOM RELATING TO MEDITATION IN A CHRISTIAN SENSE, AND WE NEED TO LEARN HOW TO DO THAT. THEN WE COME TO KNOW OURSELVES, AND THAT KNOWLEDGE OF ONE'S SELF IS GNOSIS, THIS IS THE KEY THAT UNLOCKS

THE TRUTH WITHIN OURSELVES, THAT SETS US FREE.

AS WE CAN SEE IN FIRST CORINTHIANS 2, PAUL STATES THAT WE SPEAK WISDOM AMONG THEM THAT ARE PERFECT. PERFECT IS TELEIOS, AND THOSE WHO ARE PERFECT ARE THOSE THAT ARE LIKE JESUS CHRIST.

THE WISDOM OF THOSE THAT ARE PERFECT IS NOT THE WISDOM OF THIS WORLD, IT IS NOT THE EXOTERIC LITERAL HISTORICAL WISDOM OF THIS WORLD, NOR IS IT OF THE PRINCES OF THIS WORLD, THE LEADERS OF THIS WORLD, WHICH COMES TO NOTHING, BECAUSE EVERYTHING OF THIS WORLD PASSES AWAY.

WE SPEAK THE WISDOM OF GOD IN MYSTERY, THE HIDDEN WISDOM. SO, ALL OF US MUST ENDEAVOR TO REACH THIS STAGE OF PERFECTION, THE ONE WHO ACHIEVES THAT STAGE OF PERFECTION HAS TRULY TRANSCENDED THIS CURRENT STATE; THIS IS WHAT ESOTERIC CHRISTIANITY IS SAYING IS POSSIBLE.

ESOTERIC CHRISTIANITY IS NOT JUST ANOTHER SET OF BELIEFS, IT IS NOT JUST ANOTHER SET OF PHILOSOPHICAL

MUSINGS, OR A DIFFERENT COSMOLOGY, OR A DIFFERENT WAY OF UNDERSTANDING THE CREATION OF THE UNIVERSE. ALL OF THOSE THINGS MAY BE DIFFERENT IN TERMS OF ESOTERIC CHRISTIANITY, AND WE CAN SPEAK IN MORE DEPTH IN RELATIONSHIP TO THE ORIGIN OF THE UNIVERSE, THE PHILOSOPHICAL, EPISTEMOLOGICAL VIEWS OF THE WAY WE EXPERIENCE LIFE, AND ALL SORTS OF OTHER PHILOSOPHICAL THINGS, BUT NONE OF THAT MATTERS IF WE FAIL TO LIVE THE ACTUAL LIFESTYLE, WHICH IS TO INQUIRE WITHIN OURSELVES.

WHEN WE BEGIN TO HOLD OURSELVES ACCOUNTABLE FOR ALL THE ACTIVES OF OUR MINDS AND HEARTS, THEN WE ARE BECOMING READY TO ENGAGE, TO HEAR, TO BECOME READY TO ACCEPT THE ESOTERIC TEACHINGS. SO LONG AS WE ARE BLAMING OTHERS, SO LONG AS WE CONTINUE TO BELIEVE THAT THERE IS NOTHING THAT CAN BE DONE TO CHANGE OUR INNER SELF, THEN WE ARE NOT READY.

WE WILL END THIS WITH A COUPLE OF QUOTES FROM SAMAEL AUN WEOR.

In order to understand the Bible, one needs to be a Gnostic, because the Bible is a highly symbolic book, and if we try to read it in the Protestant style, like one who reads newspaper columns, we fall into the most terrible absurdities.

— Samael Aun Weor, The Seven Words

In truth, if we read the bible literally, it doesn't make any sense, and this is enough proof to state that the literal interpretations of the Bible are incoherent.

These are the mysteries of the Gospels that must be lived here and now, within ourselves.

The life, passion, and death of our Lord Jesus Christ is not something that is strictly historic as people believe. It is something of immediate actuality that each one must perform in his or her laboratory.

This is what the crude reality of Christ is. It is not something from the history of the past that occurred two thousand years ago, it

IS SOMETHING TO BE LIVED HERE AND NOW.

— SAMAEL AUN WEOR, THE ARCHEUS

IN THIS WE HAVE JUST BEGUN TO SCRATCH THE SURFACE, WE HAVE NOT YET ACTUALLY TALKED MUCH ABOUT WHAT THIS ESOTERIC TEACHING IS. WE HAVE SIMPLY STATED THAT SUCH TEACHING EXISTS.

IN OUR FOLLOWING CHAPTERS, WE WILL BEGIN TO TEACH THE ACTUAL WAYS OF UNDERSTANDING THE BIBLE IN ORDER TO LIVE IN ACCORDANCE WITH ESOTERIC CHRISTIANITY.

# Christ, the Universal Origin

In a lecture about the esoteric path Samael Aun Weor said:

"Gnosis is the flame from which all religions sprouted, because in its depth Gnosis is religion. The word religion comes from the Latin word religare, which implies "to link the Soul to God"; so Gnosis is the very pure flame from where all religions sprout, because Gnosis is Knowledge, Gnosis is Wisdom."

With this quote we can see that analyzing the word religion reveals exactly how one should operate, what its point should really be: to link the soul to God so that the soul can experience the nature of

GOD. SOME MAY SAY THAT THIS GOES AGAINST CHRISTIANITY, BUT IF YOU LOOK IN THE RIGHT PLACE YOU CAN FIND SUPPORT FOR THIS NOTION. FOR EXAMPLE IN THE WORKS OF SAINT ATHANASIUS OF ALEXANDRIA (WHO LIVED AROUND 300AD) WROTE:

"HE [CHRIST] WAS MADE MAN THAT WE MIGHT BE MADE GOD." — SAINT ATHANASIUS OF ALEXANDRIA, De incarnatione verbi, SEC. 54.3 (CIRCA 318 AD)

IN OTHER WORDS, HE IS STATING THAT THERE IS THE POSSIBILITY THAT THE SOUL CAN UNITE WITH GOD. IN ESOTERIC CHRISTIANITY THIS IS THE WHOLE POINT: THERE IS A PATH IN ORDER TO ACHIEVE THEOSIS (THEO MEANS GOD). SO THEOSIS IS DIVINE INCARNATION, AND THROUGH THE EXPERIENCE, OR THE UNVEILING OF THIS KNOWLEDGE WITHIN US IS THE ACHIEVEMENT OF THEOSIS LITTLE BY LITTLE.

REGARDING THE OTHER PART OF THAT QUOTE, STATING THAT GNOSIS IS THE FLAME FROM WHICH ALL RELIGIONS SPROUTED, THIS IS ALSO SOMETHING THAT

SOME PEOPLE HAVE DIFFICULTY WITH. INDEED, WE ARE AFFIRMING THAT ALL WORLD RELIGIONS HAVE A TRUE COMPONENT TO THEM. CERTAINLY, IN EVERY TRADITION, IN EVERY RELIGION, WE CAN FIND FALSE INTERPRETATIONS, AND A DEGENERATION OF TRADITIONS AND IDEAS, SO THAT EVERY RELIGION CAN BECOME FANATICAL OR CAN JUST SIMPLY LOSE ITS WAY.

BUT ALSO, WE FIND THE TRUTH WITHIN EVERY GREAT RELIGION.

SAINT AUGUSTINE WRITES:

"THE VERY THING WHICH IS NOW CALLED THE CHRISTIAN RELIGION EXISTED AMONG THE ANCIENTS ALSO, NOR WAS IT WANTING FROM THE INCEPTION OF THE HUMAN RACE UNTIL THE COMING OF CHRIST IN THE FLESH, AT WHICH POINT THE TRUE RELIGION WHICH WAS ALREADY IN EXISTENCE BEGAN TO BE CALLED CHRISTIAN." — ST. AUGUSTINE, RETRACTIONES (427 AD)

LET US ALSO SEE WHAT JUSTIN MARTYR SAYS IN HIS FIRST APOLOGY:

AND WHEN WE SAY ALSO THAT THE WORD, WHO IS THE FIRST-BIRTH OF GOD,

WAS PRODUCED WITHOUT SEXUAL UNION, AND THAT HE, JESUS CHRIST, OUR TEACHER, WAS CRUCIFIED AND DIED, AND ROSE AGAIN, AND ASCENDED INTO HEAVEN, WE PROPOUND NOTHING DIFFERENT FROM WHAT YOU BELIEVE REGARDING THOSE WHOM YOU ESTEEM SONS OF JUPITER.

JUSTIN MARTYR, FIRST APOLOGY, CH. 21 (CIRCA 155 AD)

JUSTIN MARTYR HERE IS MAKING AN ANALOGY BETWEEN THE SO-CALLED PAGAN MYSTERIES AND CHRISTIAN THEOLOGY. NORMALLY MANY OF US ARE TAUGHT TO BELIEVE THAT THOSE OLD STORIES OF PAGANS WERE VERY SIMPLE, SUPERFICIAL TYPES OF THINGS, THAT HAD NOTHING AT ALL TO DO WITH TRUE RELIGION. BUT IN REALITY, THE VERY EARLY CHRISTIAN FATHERS KNEW HOW SIMILAR THE STORIES OF THE GREEK AND ROMAN GODS AND GODDESSES WERE TO THE STORIES THAT WERE EVENTUALLY WRITTEN IN THE NEW TESTAMENT.

THOSE TRADITIONS THAT WERE EVENTUALLY REPLACED BY CHRISTIANITY, ALL OF THOSE OLD RELIGIONS, THOSE

PAGAN RELIGIONS, WERE IN DECLINE AT THE TIME. THIS IS WHY THEY NEEDED TO BE REPLACED. YET, THE TRUE SOURCE OF THOSE OLD RELIGIONS IS THE SAME GNOSIS UNDERLYING ESOTERIC CHRISTIANITY. WHETHER WE CALL IT GNOSIS IN GREEK, OR SOME OTHER WORD, IT DOES NOT MATTER.

ALL TRADITIONS ARE SUSCEPTIBLE TO FALLING AWAY. WHEN A TRADITIONS USEFULNESS BEGINS TO DECLINE, NEW TRADITIONS ARE MADE IN ORDER TO RENEW THE TEACHINGS THAT LEAD TO GNOSIS, THE UNIVERSAL KNOWLEDGE WHICH ALL OF US, ALL OF OUR SOULS YEARN FOR.

ESOTERIC CHRISTIANITY IS REALLY THE TRUE UNIVERSAL DOCTRINE, THE TRUE GNOSTIC CATHOLIC DOCTRINE. AS WE HAVE SAID, CATHOLIC REALLY MEANS UNIVERSAL, AND BY GNOSTIC WE ARE TALKING ABOUT KNOWLEDGE.

GNOSIS IS THE KNOWLEDGE WE MUST POSSESS IN ORDER TO ACHIEVE THEOSIS, THE INCARNATION OF THE DIVINE. JUST LIKE THE OLD TRADITIONS OF GREECE AND ROME, AND ALL THE OTHER

TRADITIONS OF THE WORLD FALL INTO DEGENERATION, JUST AS THERE ARE GOOD AND BAD ASPECTS OF ANY TRADITION, WHEN WE TALK ABOUT GNOSTIC GROUPS, MANY GROUPS SERVED THE TRUE TEACHINGS OF CHRIST AND THERE WERE OTHER GROUPS WHICH WERE QUITE THE OPPOSITE. UNFORTUNATELY, ALL THESE GROUPS GET MIXED TOGETHER TODAY AND THIS IS PARTLY WHY A LOT OF CHRISTIANS HAVE A VERY NEGATIVE CONNOTATION OF GNOSIS.

WE HAVE TO KEEP REMINDING OURSELVES THAT GNOSIS JUST MEANS KNOWLEDGE AND THE IDEA THAT THERE IS A SPARK OF DIVINITY WITHIN US THAT CAN PROVIDE US WITH KNOWLEDGE OF THE DIVINE. THIS IS SOMETHING THAT MANY ANCIENT CHURCH FATHERS ALSO AGREED WITH. THIS IS THE FUNDAMENTAL BASIS OF GNOSIS OR GNOSTIC DOCTRINE, AND IT IS NO DIFFERENT THAN ALL OF THE TRUE ANCIENT TRADITIONS AS WELL.

WE STATED IN OUR PRIOR CHAPTER THAT CHRIST IS NOT A PERSON, BUT CHRIST IS A TYPE OF FORCE OR SUBSTANCE, AN ANIMATING PRINCIPLE, SO

WE MUST ALWAYS MAKE A DIFFERENTIATION BETWEEN THAT FORCE OF FIRE, THAT SPIRITUAL FIRE, THAT SPIRITUAL LIGHT CALLED CHRIST, AND THE ONE THAT INCARNATES THAT FIRE, THAT FORCE.

OBVIOUSLY, THE FOUNDER OF CHRISTIANITY IS JESUS CHRIST.

JESUS WAS THE NAME OF THAT INDIVIDUAL, AND CHRIST WAS THE TITLE OF THAT INDIVIDUAL, BECAUSE THAT ONE, THAT PERSON THAT WE CALL JESUS, HE DID THE WORK OF PURIFYING HIS SOUL, ACHIEVING THEOSIS TO THE MAXIMUM DEGREE, IN ORDER TO RECEIVE THE CHRIST.

WHEN JESUS RECEIVED CHRIST, HE WAS RECEIVING THE UNIVERSAL PRINCIPAL, THE UNIVERSAL INTELLIGENCE, AND WAS SPEAKING FROM THAT PERSPECTIVE SAYING, "I AM THE LIGHT OF THE WORLD." UNFORTUNATELY, PEOPLE INTERPRET THAT TO BELIEVE THAT THERE WAS ONE MANIFESTATION OF CHRIST AND THAT SINGULAR PHYSICAL MANIFESTATION AS JESUS WAS THE ONE AND ONLY CHRIST.

Actually, it is different. Anyone who achieves that level unites completely with Christ, so becomes one with Christ. Christ is universal and beyond any individual, but an individual like Jesus purifies his soul to such a degree that Christ — the Universal Force — can individualize itself into that soul, and speak and bring teachings, found religions. All the world religions are founded by Christ, different individuals who reached the level of Christ. This is what is always happening, from time to time.

According to inner or Esoteric Christianity, our role in all of this is to purify our soul, to work on our psychology, to do the inner psychological, and spiritual work.

To truly follow this teaching, we have to become practical. Many people who study religion, who are interested in these things, have a lot of theories and ideas about the differences, conceptually, of different theologies, different

MYTHOLOGIES, DIFFERENT WAYS OF UNDERSTANDING HOW GOD AND MAN INTERACT, HOW CREATION 'REALLY IS' ACCORDING TO ONE DOCTRINE OR ANOTHER. ALL OF THIS MAY HAVE SOME RELATIVE IMPORTANCE, BUT WHAT IS THE MOST IMPORTANT FOR US HERE AND NOW IS TO MAKE ESOTERIC CHRISTIANITY A PRACTICAL EFFORT IN OUR LIFE. IN ORDER TO DO THIS, WE ARE GOING TO STUDY THE BOOK OF JOHN, WE ARE GOING TO LOOK AT THE VERY BEGINNING, THE FIRST CHAPTER, THE FIRST VERSE. IT IS A VERY FAMOUS VERSE OFTEN REPEATED:

1 IN THE BEGINNING WAS THE WORD, AND THE WORD WAS WITH GOD, AND THE WORD WAS GOD.

2 THE SAME WAS IN THE BEGINNING WITH GOD.

3 ALL THINGS WERE MADE BY HIM; AND WITHOUT HIM WAS NOT ANYTHING MADE THAT WAS MADE.

4 IN HIM WAS LIFE; AND THE LIFE WAS THE LIGHT OF MEN.

5 AND THE LIGHT SHINETH IN DARKNESS; AND THE DARKNESS COMPREHENDED IT NOT.

John 1: 1 -5

Ordinarily these verses are taken in terms of a history, in terms of a historical event, something that happened many years ago, a long time ago. But, as we have stated from the esoteric viewpoint, we need to interpret all these events as a living reality within our self.

The real importance of the word esoteric, is not just that it is something hidden, but that it is hidden within our own experience. So, everything about Christianity, when you understand it from the esoteric level, is pointing to something occurring within us.

When we look at this first chapter, the first verse of John 1 "In the beginning was the Word, and the Word was with God, and the Word was God." The best way to begin to understand this is to look at some of the original Greek.

The word beginning is actually arché (pronounced arhee). This word arche is translated as the beginning,

AND NORMALLY WE LOOK AT THAT 'BEGINNING' AS A HISTORICAL EVENT. ACTUALLY, THE WAY TO UNDERSTAND THIS ESOTERICALLY, IS TO SEE THE BEGINNING AS ANOTHER WAY OF SAYING "ORIGIN".

THE ESOTERIC UNDERSTANDING OF THIS IS TO LOOK AT IT AS A CONSTANT EVENT HAPPENING WITHIN OUR SELF. SO, WHAT IS NORMALLY UNDERSTOOD AS "IN THE BEGINNING" WE CAN SAY IS "AT THE ORIGIN," OR "IN THE ORIGIN."

WHERE DOES ANYTHING BEGIN? IT BEGINS AT THE ORIGIN, SO ANOTHER WAY TO UNDERSTAND ARCHÉ IS TO SAY THE ORIGIN. SO, INSTEAD OF ARCHÉ BEING INTERPRETED AS A HISTORICAL PAST, IT IS SEEN AS THE POINT, THE ORIGIN, THE PLACE, AND THAT ORIGIN AGAIN ESOTERICALLY, WE ARE LOOKING FOR SOMETHING INSIDE OF OURSELVES, BECAUSE WE, AS A SOUL IS CONNECTED TO OUR SPIRIT, AND OUR SPIRIT IS CONNECTED TO CHRIST.

THEREFORE, IN THE BEGINNING, OR AT THE ORIGIN, WAS THE WORD. WORD IS Λόγος, LOGOS IN GREEK, SOMETIMES IT IS ALSO TRANSLATED AS VERB. A VERB IS AN

ACTIVITY. MANY TIMES, LOGOS IN GREEK IS USED TO TALK ABOUT LOGIC AND REASONING, BUT IN THIS SENSE, THIS IS NOT WHAT WE ARE POINTING TOWARDS. THIS LOGOS MENTIONED HERE IS VERY MUCH BEYOND ANYTHING WE NORMALLY SEE AS INTELLECT OR REASONING. THE INTELLECT OR REASONING IS AN ACTIVITY OF OUR MIND. WE MUST SEARCH DEEPER THAN THE MIND, BEYOND THE MIND.

WHAT WE ARE REALLY POINTING TO HERE WITH THIS LOGOS IS THE VERY PRIMORDIAL ACTIVITY, THE PRIMARY CAUSE, THAT EMERGES FROM THE RADICAL ORIGIN.

THEREFORE, FROM AN ESOTERIC UNDERSTANDING, IN THE BEGINNING WAS THE WORD, IS BETTER STATED WITHIN THE ORIGIN IS THE PRIMORDIAL ACTIVITY.

CONTINUING WITH THIS UNDERSTANDING, WE CAN SAY, "WITHIN THE ORIGIN IS THE PRIMORDIAL ACTIVITY, AND THE PRIMORDIAL ACTIVITY IS WITH GOD, AND THE PRIMORDIAL ACTIVITY IS GOD."

If we do not understand this correctly one might think that this interpretation is implying that we are Gods, because we are saying within our primordial activity is God. We must understand this in a very subtle and refined sense. Obviously, our current condition is very far away from God, we should never forget that. But we must also remember that theosis is possible, that our soul can unite with God, that our soul arrived from God. What our soul is today, what we are today, arrived from that primordial activity, which is Christ, and through a profound work, through an inner work we can reunite with Christ in gnosis.

Arche is an interesting word. We find a lot of other words that come from it such as Archangel, which is a principle or chief angel, an original angel, an angel that is emanating that Arch. In other words, an Archangel is superior to that of a regular Angel because it has fully

OR MORE DEVELOPED THAT ARCHE, THAT ORIGINAL ACTIVITY, IT IS CLOSER TO THAT ORIGIN.

THERE IS ALSO A WORD USED A LOT CALLED ARCHETYPE. ARCHETYPE MEANS A PRIMORDIAL MOLD. AN ARCHETYPE IS LIKE A BLUEPRINT FOR SOMETHING THAT MUST BE DEVELOPED WITHIN OUR SELF. WE HAVE THESE POTENTIAL CONNECTIONS, LIKE I SAID PRIOR, OUR SOUL IS CONNECTED TO OUR SPIRIT AND OUR SPIRIT IS CONNECTED TO CHRIST, AND CHRIST IS MANIFESTED IN MANY DIFFERENT ARCHETYPES, MANY DIFFERENT WAYS IN WHICH THE LIGHT IS FORMED.

WHEN THESE ARCHETYPES MANIFEST THEMSELVES, WHEN THESE ARCHETYPES ARE DEVELOPED CORRECTLY, THEN ALL OF THE BEAUTIFUL QUALITIES OF THE SOUL ARE MANIFEST AND ALL THOSE QUALITIES OF ANY RELIGIOUS SAINT OR PROPHET APPEAR. ALL OF THOSE AMAZING, WONDERFUL QUALITIES ARE MANIFESTATIONS OF THE ARCHETYPES.

UNFORTUNATELY, WHAT WE HAVE WITHIN OURSELVES IS A WRONG DEVELOPMENT OF THOSE ARCHETYPES.

What we have within ourselves can be understood in terms of the passions. Many monks and contemplatives of the Christian religion will talk about the passions. From a modern prospective we talk about the same thing as ego, the egotistical desires. Any egotistical desire is a type of energy that influences our behavior. But this energy comes about because of our prior actions. It is like a pattern of energy, and every time similar circumstances come in front of us in the world, there are times in which these passions, these patterns of energy, come forth and we end up acting in ways which are very far away from our religious ideals.

Today a lot of times people do not know how to deal with these things. In order to make this doctrine practical we must look at the origin of all of our activity. Because within that radical origin we will find Christ, we will find the gnosis, the knowledge that shall bring us

TOWARDS THEOSIS, THE INCARNATION OF THE DIVINE.

IN ORDER TO DO THIS, WE NEED TO LOOK, WE NEED TO PLACE OUR ATTENTION, OUR OBSERVATION, WITHIN OUR MIND AND WITHIN OUR HEART. WE MUST SEE THE WAY THAT WE ACTUALLY BEHAVE. WE MUST BEGIN TO CONTEMPLATE THE WAY IN WHICH OUR MIND ACTUALLY WORKS. IT IS NOT ENOUGH TO BE REPENTANT OF SOME POOR DECISION, OR SOME POOR ACTION, THAT CAME FORTH. IT IS GOOD, AND IT IS EVEN NECESSARY, BUT IT IS NOT ENOUGH. WE MUST COME TO KNOW OUR OWN DARKNESS, OUR OWN SINS.

GOD GIVES US THE CAPACITY TO KNOW OUR SELF, AND THROUGH THAT RELATIONSHIP OF STRUGGLING TO WORK ON OUR SELF, AND ASKING FOR HELP, LITTLE BY LITTLE, THE LORD GIVES US THE LIGHT. ONLY THROUGH THE PROCESS OF LEARNING FROM OUR MISTAKES TO WE BECOME VERY WISE. THE LORD IS NOT INTERESTED IN AN IGNORANT PERSON, THE LORD WANTS WISDOM, LOVE, COMPASSION. IN ORDER TO INHABIT

THOSE QUALITIES, THAT WE MUST LOOK INSIDE OF OURSELVES, WE HAVE TO LOOK AT OUR OWN EGO, OUR OWN PASSIONS.

IF WE SIT DOWN, WE REST, WE CLOSE OUR EYES, WE RELAX, WHAT DO WE SEE?

WHAT ACTIVITY DO YOU SEE?

FOR MOST OF US IF YOU HAVE JUST DONE THIS FOR THE FIRST TIME YOU WILL FIND SOMETHING.

YOU WILL REALIZE THAT YOUR MIND CONTINUES EVEN THOUGH YOU DO NOT WISH IT TO. YOU WILL FIND THAT YOU HAVE EMOTIONS THAT HAVE NO GOOD PLACE WITHIN YOU. YOU HAVE ENMITY TOWARDS OTHERS, JEALOUSY, LUST, HATRED. PERHAPS YOU WORRY. PERHAPS YOUR MIND CONTINUES TO THINK EVEN WHEN YOU DO NOT WANT TO THINK. ALL OF THIS IS ACTIVITY. ALL OF THIS HAS SOME ORIGIN. IT IS YOUR DUTY TO DISCOVER IT.

NOTICE THAT YOU HAVE THE CAPABILITY TO SEE IT, THAT YOU ARE THE WATCHER. YOU ARE NOTICING IT, WHICH MEANS YOU DO NOT HAVE TO BE AUTOMATICALLY PULLED INTO DOING ANYTHING. YOU CAN SEE YOUR MIND ACTING ON ITS OWN ACCORD.

This is exactly what the passions are. They seem to act even though we do not want them to. This is what we call the ego, but the ego is really egos, many different things many different activities that erupt from moment to moment without our slightest endorsement. They arrive upon their own accord and they seem to do whatever they want. Normally we think that is who we truly are. Someone says some bad words to us, and we immediately become insulted or hurt, and that activity of hurt or feeling insulted, we believe, that is who we truly are. We are always thinking that whatever activity arises in our mind must be an expression of our 'perfect' self.

But actually, most of what occurs in our mind is imperfection. Things arrive in our mind based on no good reason. The way that we act, the way that we behave reinforces all of these patterns of behavior. The way we behave, the way our mind reacts

TO THE WORLD, TELLS US SOMETHING ABOUT OUR SELF. NORMALLY WE BELIEVE THAT WHAT IS GOING ON IN OUR MIND SAYS SOMETHING ABOUT THE OTHER PERSON, BUT ESOTERICALLY WHAT IT MEANS IS THAT IT IS SOMETHING ABOUT OUR SELF. THE WAY THAT WE BEHAVE IS ALWAYS COMING FROM WITHIN.

CERTAINLY, THE MIND IS RESPONDING TO SOMETHING IN THE ENVIRONMENT, BUT TWO PEOPLE EXPERIENCING THE SAME ENVIRONMENT WILL REACT DIFFERENTLY. THEREFORE, THE ORIGIN, THE RADICAL ORIGIN OF THE ACTIVITY EMERGING FROM THOSE TWO PEOPLE IS NOT FROM THE OUTSIDE WORLD. THERE IS A RELATIONSHIP THERE, BUT THE RADICAL ORIGIN IS ALWAYS WITHIN. THEREFORE, ALL OF THIS ACTIVITY WHICH IS EMERGING FROM US MUST BE SEEN FOR WHAT IT IS, WHICH IS USUALLY JUST NONSENSE, SOME IMPERFECT WAY OF BEING.

JESUS SAID THAT WE MUST BECOME PERFECT AS OUR FATHER IN HEAVEN IS PERFECT. THIS IS THE GOAL. DO NOT BE CONFUSED, THAT IS EXACTLY THE GOAL. BUT THE MESSAGE THAT IS EVERYWHERE

TODAY IS THAT SUCH A GOAL IS A FALLACY, A SOPHISM, AN IMPRACTICALITY. THE MESSAGE EXPRESSED EVERYWHERE TODAY IS THAT WE ARE JUST FILTHY ANIMALS AND WE SHOULD JUST ENGORGE OURSELVES, THAT IF WE FEEL LUST WE SHOULD JUST ENGAGE IN LUST, WE SHOULD JUST FIND THINGS TO ENGORGE OUR MIND IN. SOME ACTIVITY ERUPTS IN OUR MIND AND WANTS SOMETHING AND THE BEST WAY TO DEAL WITH IT IS TO JUST ENGAGE IN IT AND DEVELOP IT MORE. THAT WE SHOULD HAVE 'HEALTHY' AND 'WHOLESOME' EGOTISTICAL DESIRES.

BUT THE TRUTH IS EVERY ACTIVITY THAT EMERGES, IF IT IS BASED ON IGNORANCE AND WE ENGAGE IN IT, WE WILL SUFFER. IF OUR LIFE IS FULL OF SUFFERING IT IS BECAUSE WE ARE IGNORANT OF THE TRUE CAUSE OF THAT SUFFERING, AND EVERY TIME WE REENGAGE IN SOME ACTIVITY THAT WE BELIEVE BRINGS HAPPINESS, BUT ACTUALLY BRINGS SUFFERING, WE REINFORCE THESE PATTERNS UNTIL THEY BECOME VERY STRONG.

EVERY TIME WE PLACATE OUR FEARS, INSTEAD OF ANALYZING THEM, WE

REINFORCE THE FEAR. AND THE NEXT TIME THAT FEAR HAS AN OPPORTUNITY TO ARRIVE, IT WILL COME BACK STRONGER. EVERY TIME WE ENGAGE AND SATISFY OUR LUSTS, THE NEXT TIME THAT LUST HAS AN OPPORTUNITY TO BECOME ACTIVE IN OUR PSYCHE IT WILL BE STRONGER. IF YOU KEEP FOLLOWING THAT OVER AND OVER AGAIN, YOU BUILD A STATE OF MIND WHICH HAS ZERO FREEDOM. WHEN WE HAVE A RIGID, CAGED MIND, EVERYTHING CAUSES AN ENORMOUS ERUPTION, AND THE PERSON LIVES A VERY CHAOTIC LIFE, ALWAYS COMPELLED TO ACT, ALWAYS A SLAVE TO EVERY IMPRESSION THAT APPEARS, NEVER HAVING ANY TRUE FREE WILL, NEVER HAVING ANY OPPORTUNITY FOR HAPPINESS. THIS TYPE OF PERSON, WHICH IS ALL OF US BASICALLY, USUALLY RESORTS TO ATTEMPTING TO CONTROL THE OUTSIDE WORLD IN SUCH A WAY THAT THEIR MIND WILL BE SATISFIED, BUT IT NEVER ACTUALLY WORKS.

IN OUR PREVIOUS CHAPTER WE TALKED ABOUT NEEDING TO ADOPT A CONTEMPLATIVE LIFESTYLE, BUT BY THIS WE ARE NOT TALKING ABOUT

DISENGAGING FROM OUR PRACTICAL LIFE AND GOING INTO THE FOREST OR INTO THE MOUNTAINS. CERTAINLY, THAT TYPE OF LIFE OR RETREAT IS GOOD, IN ITS OWN WAY, BUT IN THIS MODERN ERA WE HAVE TO COMBINE OUR PRACTICAL DAILY LIFE, AS IT IS, WITH THESE CONTEMPLATIVE THEMES, TO INTEGRATE A CONTEMPLATION OF OUR DAILY LIFE.

THIS MEANS TO BEGIN TO REFLECT AND BEGIN TO MEDITATE ON OUR LIFE, AS IT IS HERE AND NOW. ALL OF OUR IMPRESSIONS OF OUR ORDINARY WORLD PROVIDE ALL THE ERUPTIONS OF ACTIVITY FROM OUR MIND THAT WE NEED TO COMPREHEND. IT IS NOT NECESSARY TO RUN AWAY FROM LIFE. WHAT IS NECESSARY IS TO ANALYZE, TO REFLECT, TO CONTEMPLATE, TO MEDITATE ON ALL THE THINGS THAT ARE ARRIVING IN OUR MIND.

NORMALLY EVERYTHING THAT ARRIVES IN OUR MIND, WE SEE AS SOMETHING THAT HAPPENED "OUT THERE" IN THE EXTERNAL WORLD. WE DO NOT RECOGNIZE THAT IT IS ACTUALLY OUR MIND THAT IS REACTING; WE THINK THAT SOMETHING HAPPENED,

AND IMMEDIATELY IT WAS TERRIBLE, THAT WE ARE JUST FORCED TO BE DEPRESSED ABOUT IT. BUT ACTUALLY, IT IS OUR STATE OF MIND THAT WAS ATTACHED TO SOME CIRCUMSTANCE IN LIFE, AND WHEN THAT CIRCUMSTANCE CHANGED, IT WAS OUR MIND THAT WAS ATTACHED TO IT THAT SUFFERS.

EVERY TIME WE FEEL INTENSE SUFFERING IT IS AN OPPORTUNITY TO KNOW THE TRUTH ABOUT OUR SELF.

INSTEAD OF TAKING EVERY DIFFICULTY IN LIFE AS SOME OBSTACLE TO YOUR HAPPINESS, TAKE IT AS THE PATH DIRECTLY TO YOUR HAPPINESS.

UNPLEASANT MANIFESTATIONS ARE SHOWING YOU SOMETHING ABOUT YOUR MIND, AN EXTREME LEVEL OF ACTIVITY WITHIN YOU, THAT BEFOREHAND YOU DID NOT HAVE THE OPPORTUNITY TO SEE. WHAT YOU MUST COME TO KNOW IS THAT YOU HAVE A SPARK OF DIVINITY WITHIN YOU, AND NO MATTER WHAT HAPPENS YOU WILL ALWAYS HAVE THAT, YOU WILL ALWAYS HAVE THE CAPABILITY OF OBSERVING YOURSELF AT ANY MOMENT, AT ANY SPONTANEOUS MOMENT YOU CAN

OBSERVE YOUR MIND. FROM THAT BASIS, THAT IS THE MUSTARD SEED OF FAITH, AND BY FAITH HERE WE MEAN DIRECTLY EXPERIENCING YOUR MIND. YOU CAN DIRECTLY EXPERIENCE YOUR MIND.

WHEN YOU CAN OBSERVE IT, YOU CAN SEE ITS ACTIVITY AND IN COMBINATION WITH PRAYER YOU CAN TRANSFORM YOUR PSYCHOLOGY. YOU MUST HAVE A TRUE REPENTANCE FOR THE EVILS YOU HAVE INFLICTED, FOR THE SUFFERINGS THAT YOU HAVE INFLICTED UPON THE WORLD, FOR YOUR INABILITY, YOUR INCAPABILITY OF UPHOLDING THE CHRISTIAN ETHIC, YOU MUST FEEL THE REMORSE FOR THAT, YOU MUST ACKNOWLEDGE THAT YOU HAVE ACTED IN THE WRONG WAY.

YOU MUST CONFESS YOUR SINS, BUT YOU DO NOT NEED TO CONFESS IT TO SOMEONE ELSE, YOU MUST CONFESS IT WITHIN YOURSELF. YOU MUST PRAY TO THE LORD AND CONFESS YOUR SINS DAILY, WITH TRUE REPENTANCE. BUT YOU MUST DO MORE THAN JUST ASK FOR FORGIVENESS, YOU MUST SEE HOW THAT ACTIVITY ARRIVED, WHY YOU CHOSE TO DO WHAT YOU DID, WHY THE IMPULSE OF

YOUR MIND ARRIVED IN YOU. YOU TOOK THE WRONG PATH, YOU TOOK THE WRONG CHOICE, WHY? PERHAPS YOU TAKE A SELFISH WAY, AN EASY WAY... PERHAPS WE FEEL HURT, SO WE HURT ANOTHER PERSON.

ALL OF THIS IS WRONG AND WE KNOW IT IS WRONG, SO PAY ATTENTION TO IT, LOOK WITHIN YOURSELF, ACKNOWLEDGE ITS EXISTENCE, SEE THE ORIGIN OF THAT WRONG ACTIVITY AND FROM THAT BASIS SEE HOW YOU COULD HAVE DONE IT CORRECTLY, SEE WHERE SUCH A NOTION, OR SUCH A WRONG IMPULSE ARRIVED IN THE FIRST PLACE, ASK FOR ASSISTANCE, PRAY. DO ALL THOSE THINGS DAILY AND YOUR MIND WILL TRANSFORM, YOUR HEART WILL TRANSFORM.

UNFORTUNATELY AS MUCH AS PEOPLE SAY THEY WANT TO BE A GOOD CHRISTIAN THEY DO NOT TAKE THE EFFORT PRACTICALLY, THEY JUST WANT TO PRAY ON SUNDAY, THEY WANT TO GIVE GLORY TO GOD ON SUNDAY, BUT THEN THEY BEHAVE IN ALL SORTS OF OTHER WAYS AND WHEN THEY DO WRONG ACTIONS.

We often ignore their wrong actions, and if they are confronted, we justify, we say we had to act that way. All of this is laziness which prevents us from entering honestly into the esoteric doctrine. To be truly prepared for the esoteric doctrine we must be prepared to look radically within ourselves at every moment to acknowledge the imperfection that we have.

We must want to change that imperfection, we must know that it is possible to change that imperfection, because what lies within us at the root is that teleios (perfection), which Paul speaks about.

Paul says, "Howbeit we speak wisdom among them that are perfect..." (1 Corinthians 2:6). This is not a perfection of the ego; this is a perfection of the Glory of God manifesting the Light of Christ.

Beyond our personality, affections, and mind, beyond our individuality, is the Light of Christ,

THE GLORY OF CHRIST, THE WISDOM OF CHRIST. THAT IS OUR ROOT, AND THAT IS WHAT WE MUST WORK TO MANIFEST IN THE WORLD.

THIS IS ESOTERIC CHRISTIANITY.

YOURS IN LOVE AND LIGHT,
FRATER L.V.X.e.T
OCTAVES DRAGONFLY

# QUOTES

Magick is the science and art of causing change to occur in conformity with will.
Aleister Crowley


Movies will end up being this esoteric art form, where only singular people will put films out in a small group of theaters.
M. Night Shyamalan


In mystical traditions, it is one's own readiness that makes experiences exoteric or esoteric. The secret isn't that you're not being told. The secret is that you're not able to hear.
This quote copyright © By Pumpkin Limited
Ram Dass

Esoteric philosophy teaches that the physical form, the body, of the individual is made new at birth; but the soul is ancient, the stuff of stars.
Normandi Ellis


Eschew the ordinary, disdain the commonplace
Chuck Jones


The grain of real knowledge is concealed in a vast deal of esoteric chaff.
Alfred Rupert Hall


It is an esoteric doctrine of society, that a little wickedness is good to make muscle; as if conscience were not good for hands and legs.
Ralph Waldo Emerson

We are so busy and have become so complex, being simple is actually esoteric.
Bryan Kest

When we become expert in something, our tastes grow more esoteric and complex.
Malcolm Gladwell

The Occultists, however, know that the traditions of Esoteric Philosophy must be the right ones, simply because they are the most logical, and reconcile every difficulty.
H. P. Blavatsky

If God does not exist, and if religion is an illusion that the majority of men cannot live without ... let men believe in the lies of religion since they cannot do without them, and let

THEN A HANDFUL OF SAGES, WHO
KNOW THE TRUTH AND CAN LIVE WITH
IT, KEEP IT AMONG THEMSELVES. MEN
ARE THEN DIVIDED INTO THE WISE
AND THE FOOLISH, THE
PHILOSOPHERS AND THE COMMON
MEN, AND ATHEISM BECOMES A
GUARDED, ESOTERIC DOCTRINE - FOR
IF THE ILLUSIONS OF RELIGION WERE
TO BE DISCREDITED, THERE IS NO
TELLING WITH WHAT MADNESS MEN
WOULD BE SEIZED, WITH WHAT
UNCONTROLLABLE ANGUISH.
IRVING KRISTOL


ABSTRACTION IS AN ESOTERIC
LANGUAGE.
ERIC FISCHL


WHEN YOGA IS UNDERSTOOD IN ITS
TOTALITY, IT IS NEITHER A FORM OF
EXERCISE, NOR IS IT AN ESOTERIC
PHILOSOPHY OR RELIGION; IT IS A
PRACTICAL AND COMPREHENSIVE

SCIENCE FOR REALIZING LIFE'S ULTIMATE AIMS.
  ROD STRYKER

  LIFE IS A DESERT OF SHIFTING SAND DUNES. UNPREDICTABLE. ERRATIC. HARMONY CHANGES INTO DISSONANCE, THE IMMEDIATE OUTLIVES THE PROFOUND, ESOTERIC BECOMES CLICHED. AND VICE VERSA.
  ELLA LEYA

  DEEP DOWN, YOU SEE, I LONG TO BE ARCANE, ESOTERIC. I WOULD LOVE TO CONFOUND PEOPLE WITH THEIR OWN LANGUAGE.
  DAVID LEVITHAN

  IT IS TRUE THAT SOME SECLUDED INTELLECTUALS IN THEIR ESOTERIC CIRCLES TALK DIFFERENTLY. THEY PROCLAIM THE PRIORITY OF WHAT THEY CALL ETERNAL ABSOLUTE VALUES AND FEIGN IN THEIR

DECLAMATIONS—NOT IN THEIR PERSONAL CONDUCT—A DISDAIN OF THINGS SECULAR AND TRANSITORY. BUT THE PUBLIC IGNORES SUCH UTTERANCES. THE MAIN GOAL OF PRESENT-DAY POLITICAL ACTION IS TO SECURE FOR THE RESPECTIVE PRESSURE GROUP MEMBERSHIPS THE HIGHEST MATERIAL WELL-BEING. THE ONLY WAY FOR A LEADER TO SUCCEED IS TO INSTILL IN PEOPLE THE CONVICTION THAT HIS PROGRAM BEST SERVES THE ATTAINMENT OF THIS GOAL.

LUDWIG VON MISES

IN ALL FORMS OF MAGICK, THE IMAGINATION OR IMAGE-MAKING FACULTY IS THE MOST IMPORTANT FACTOR

KENNETH GRANT

A TIME COMES WHEN IT ISN'T ENOUGH TO READ ABOUT BUDDHA,

WE WISH TO HAVE THAT HAPPEN TO OURSELVES. THAT'S WHEN WE MOVE FROM THE EXOTERIC TO THE ESOTERIC, FROM RELIGION TO MYSTICISM.
  FREDERICK LENZ


ESOTERIC SCIENCE PREMISES THE EXISTENCE OF THE GREAT UNMANIFEST, WHICH MAY BE CONCEIVED AS A SEA OF LIMITLESS BUT LATENT FORCE WHICH UNDERLIES ALL THINGS AND WHENCE ALL THINGS DERIVE THEIR SUBSTANCE AND DRAW THEIR LIFE.
  DION FORTUNE


THE SECRET DOCTRINE IS THE COMMON PROPERTY OF THE COUNTLESS MILLIONS OF MEN BORN UNDER VARIOUS CLIMATES, IN TIMES WITH WHICH HISTORY REFUSES TO DEAL, AND TO WHICH ESOTERIC TEACHINGS ASSIGN DATES

INCOMPATIBLE WITH THE THEORIES
OF GEOLOGY AND ANTHROPOLOGY.
  H. P. BLAVATSKY

  TO AVERT THE DANGER [POSED BY
THEORY] TO LIFE, NIETZSCHE COULD
CHOOSE ONE OF TWO WAYS: HE
COULD INSIST ON THE STRICTLY
ESOTERIC CHARACTER OF THE
THEORETICAL ANALYSIS OF LIFE -
THAT IS, RESTORE THE PLATONIC
NOTION OF THE NOBLE DELUSION -
OR ELSE HE COULD DENY THE
POSSIBILITY OF THEORY PROPER AND
SO CONCEIVE OF THOUGHT AS
ESSENTIALLY SUBSERVIENT TO, OR
DEPENDENT ON, LIFE OR FATE... IF
NOT NIETZSCHE HIMSELF, AT ANY
RATE HIS SUCCESSORS [HEIDEGGER]
ADOPTED THE SECOND ALTERNATIVE.
  LEO STRAUSS

The blunt large questions
become connected to smaller,
apparently esoteric ones.
   Alain de Botton


   Christian scholars often say
that Sufi theories are close to
those of Christianity. Many
Moslems maintain that they are
essentially derived from Islam.
The resemblance of many Sufi
ideas to those of several
religious and esoteric systems
are sometimes taken as evidence
of derivation. The Islamic
interpretation is that religion is
of one origin, differences being
due to local or historical
causes.
   Idries Shah


   Nearly all spiritual practices
are based on attention. In fact,
whenever you think you have

LOST THE PATH, OR WHENEVER YOU
FEEL CONFUSED BY ESOTERIC
TERMINOLOGY OR TECHNIQUE,
REMEMBER THAT ALL THESE
TECHNIQUES OR TEACHINGS ARE
VARIOUS WAYS TO HELP YOU LEARN
TO PAY ATTENTION.
  RICK FIELDS

  I HATE TO SOUND ESOTERIC, BUT
THERE IS SOMETHING ABOUT A HOUSE
THAT LEADS YOU TO THAT ONE CHAIR,
THAT ONE CORNER, WHERE YOU JUST
SIT AND FEEL COMFORTABLE.
  FRANCISCO COSTA

www.ingramcontent.com/pod-product-compliance
Lightning Source LLC
Chambersburg PA
CBHW021039160726

47994CB00006B/2634